Healthy Habits,
Happy Kids

Healthy Habits, Happy Kids

A Practical Plan to Help Your Family

Gregory L. Jantz, Ph.D.

with Ann McMurray

Revell
Grand Rapids, Michigan

© 2005 by Gregory L. Jantz

Published by Fleming H. Revell
a division of Baker Publishing Group
P.O. Box 6287, Grand Rapids, MI 49516-6287

Printed in the United States of America

Library of Congress Cataloging-in-Publication Data
Jantz, Gregory L.
    Healthy habits, happy kids : a practical plan to help your family / Gregory L. Jantz, with Ann McMurray.
        p.   cm.
    Includes bibliographical references.
    ISBN 0-8007-3078-X (pbk.)
    1. Child rearing—Religious aspects—Christianity. 2. Christian children—Health and hygiene. I. McMurray, Ann. II. Title
BV4529.J35 2006
248.8'45—dc22   2005020393

Contents

Introduction

From Weight to Worth

This book is about kids but written to parents. It's about childhood, but it's also about the adult world within which childhood exists. This book is about weight, but it's also about worth and value. It's about your child, and it's also about your family. When I say it's written to parents, I mean to include all those who have the privilege to care for children, be they grandparents, guardians, stepparents, or extended family. To paraphrase Psalm 127:4–5, children are a blessing from the Lord! And with that blessing comes God's charge to love and care for them. With that blessing comes God's promise to be with you. And you'll need it, because raising kids today can be a challenge.

Somewhere along the line, kids have lost some of their childhood. We've taken it from them through our accelerated culture. We've overshadowed it by adult concerns and worries. Through a long line of stress-induced choices, we keep putting their childhood on hold. The sum of our daily decisions can add up to a childhood compromised or lost.

That certainly isn't our intent as parents, but it's becoming a common outcome.

Changes in our culture and society have negatively impacted the health and well-being of kids today. Our kids are more stressed, less connected, more busy, and less active than we were growing up. As parents, we see this but feel at a loss to know how to regain control over our own frenetic lifestyles and return a healthy, balanced childhood to our kids. Concerned with our own weight, we worry over the physical health of our kids, as childhood weight gain and obesity levels begin to mirror adult epidemic proportions. Caught between the dangers of unhealthy weight on one hand and the dangers of unhealthy attitudes about weight, food, and body image on the other, parents are left struggling. We want to help but don't know how. Sometimes what you do to try to help just ends up making the whole situation worse. So you do nothing, out of fear, which provides no solution at all.

> Our kids are more **stressed,** less connected, more busy, and less active.

But we must provide a solution! Our kids are being weighed down not just with extra pounds but with conditions and concerns long thought to be strictly associated with adulthood and advancing age: hypertension, type 2 diabetes, high cholesterol, anxiety, and stress. Given these realities, we want our children to lose weight and live healthy and happy lives.

Helping Kids SOAR

The secret to healthy kids can be found through a whole-person approach to the needs of your child. Each child is more than he or she weighs. Each is a compilation of preferences, personality, genetics, and family patterns. In society today, appearance takes center stage, but a thin child is not necessarily a healthy child. By addressing the emotional, relational, physical, and spiritual needs of children, parents are able to provide a balanced, caring environment that contributes to lifelong happiness and health.

I call this helping a child to SOAR. As parents, we must strive to allow our children to grow up in an environment where they are

Supported—provided intentional guidance, direction, and nurturing

Optimistic—assured of a bright hope and future ahead for them as they grow

Active and Achieving—finding success in their personal and family endeavors and in active, energetic pursuits

Responsible—understanding and accepting their own part in healthy living and choices

When children grow up with this framework, they are truly able to SOAR through a healthy, happy childhood and into a productive, vital adulthood.

Helping Your Child SOAR Emotionally

As you assist your child in attaining physical goals, you must determine where your child is emotionally. In our culture, adults use food as a way to deal with the stresses and uncertainties of life. Our kids may do the same, since they can be as caught up in this fast-paced, stressful life as we are. Food can become pleasure, reward, companion, rebellion, or sheer comfort. You need to understand what your child needs emotionally and how he or she may be turning to food to obtain it. Your child's needs are not wrong, but if food has become his or her primary source of meeting those needs, you must intervene as a parent. You can intentionally provide for those needs in non-food ways and return food to its proper place as nutrition for growing, active children. You can return food to being the ally, not the enemy, of your child today and for the future.

Helping Your Child SOAR Relationally

Children need parents around them who believe in their child's bright future, who sacrifice themselves for the child's well-being. Children need adult examples of how to get along together, of what's really important, of how to handle the inevitable setbacks in life, of integrating defeats and victories today into life tomorrow. Children need stability, love, and acceptance. As a parent, you are able to provide this vital foundation. A child who feels loved and accepted is less likely to turn to counterfeits for significance and more likely to find the courage to assimilate needed changes. Love and acceptance bring freedom to grow and to change.

Helping Your Child SOAR Physically

Running, jumping, and playing are synonymous with childhood. Or are they? Have running, jumping, and playing been replaced by television, video games, and the computer in your child's life? Sedentary lifestyles used to be only for tired, worn-out adults. More and more children, however, are succumbing to inactive, snack-driven habits. As parents, we have the imperative to restructure our children's surroundings and activities to reflect a healthy balance of physical activity, exercise, and fun. Your child needs to be active, to use and stretch and grow that miraculous body given by God—for life. You can help your child integrate healthy eating and activities into his or her life right now and into adulthood.

Have running, jumping, and playing been replaced by

Helping Your Child SOAR Spiritually

Your child is a spiritual being, with an innate understanding of and faith in God. These attributes of childhood are precious and fragile. They can be damaged by the very people—parents—who desire them so desperately for their children. Undergirding a healthy, balanced life for every child is a firm foundation of knowing who he or she is to God. Parents have a special responsibility to teach and affirm this faith. Concepts of self-worth, true value, forgiveness, and acceptance cannot be adequately taught without a framework of spiritual instruction. Parents are permitted and expected by God to pass along God's love to their children. Your child needs to learn faith from you and needs to see that faith expressed in your own life.

SOAR-ing Starts with Your Support

Once you realize the diverse needs of your child, you may find it daunting to think you could ever fulfill them! But you can and you must. You are not alone, and you don't have to be perfect. All God expects is that you lean on him and do your very best. You can gain his counsel through prayer, Scripture, and the support of godly family and friends.

If each person waited to become a parent until he or she understood everything perfectly, none of us would be here today! You became a parent out of a desire to love and nurture another special human being, your child, hopeful that you would find the encouragement, strength, and support you needed along the way. Nothing has changed! Allow your ongoing love for your child and desire for his or her well-being to motivate you to do your very best to provide for these needs. Step out in faith and let God lead the way.

television, video games, and the computer in your child's life?

In order to give your child a healthy, balanced life, you must live one yourself. With children, you will be completely ineffective saying, *Do as I say but not as I do.* No matter how much you say, children will model what you do. Your behavior affects the validity of your words. Say you love him but don't act like it, and your child will doubt your affection. Say it's important to eat healthy but keep all the unhealthy food for your own consumption, and your child will continue to covet those foods. Say it's fun to exercise but make no effort to be physically active or always complain when you are and your child will lose motivation. Your attitude counts! Your example counts! The more sedentary and weighed down you are, the harder it will be for your child to SOAR.

> In order to give your child a healthy, balanced life, you must live one yourself.

This is not to say that those with physical infirmities or challenges are unable to raise healthy children. I have seen enough successful families in this situation to know otherwise. Yet many parents have come to my office concerned about the same things in their children that they are concerned about in themselves: excess weight, lack of motivation, unhappiness, and difficulty with peers. Since the child lives within the context of the family, the answers must be provided within the family context also.

For this reason a healthy, balanced life is important for all members of the family, no matter the age or physical condition. The effort will be undermined if one or more family members consider themselves "above" making the necessary dietary and lifestyle changes. When all members of the family are joined together and committed to a common goal, each member is supported by the others. Remember, *support* is what gets SOAR off the ground!

Turning Your Own Issues Over to God

Because this effort is so important to your child and to your family, you will need to spend time with God each day, turning over your own issues with change, convenience, food, weight, and body image to him. You will need to be prepared, committed, and motivated for these positive changes to succeed, especially when the going gets rough. For your child's sake, don't kid yourself as to how hard this will be. Entrenched family patterns are difficult to overcome. You may be dealing not only with your current family's patterns but also with the family patterns of yourself and your spouse. Negative self-talk from your past has a way of blurting out under stress and poisoning your efforts. You will need to guard yourself spiritually, through prayer and study. Taking hold of God's help, wisdom, and strength will allow you to approach these changes in a positive and optimistic manner.

Setting the Stage for Success

Before you begin, you'll want to spend some time in honest appraisal of your own and your child's lifestyle choices. How did you get to where you are and why? What are the factors in play? Who else is involved? Understanding where you are right now and how you got there can help you achieve long-term success. We will focus on this evaluation in chapter 1.

Understanding where you are
right now
and how you got there
can help you achieve
long-term
success.

Preparing Yourself for the Long-Term

We live in a fast-food, fast-paced society, where meals can be obtained in under five minutes and solutions found by the end of an hour-long television show. We've come to expect that if we feel really, *really* strongly about something, we should be able to fix it—and fast. We don't like waiting. Once we've identified a problem, we want it to go away quickly. This isn't going to happen without significant, long-term lifestyle changes. They are by nature difficult to alter. They require time, patience, and perseverance—a little like parenting in general. Prepare yourself by having realistic goals and a timetable for seeing progress on those goals. You may even need to redefine your idea of progress. This is no time for perfectionism. Your child needs your constant, unwavering support, not your frantic, desperate desire to have the problem go away so you can feel better about yourself as a parent.

> Have realistic goals and a timetable for progress.

Taking Flight to SOAR

Creating a healthy and balanced environment for your child to SOAR revolves around four interconnected elements. Here is how you can SOAR yourself: make sure your child feels supported by you (support); communicate your belief in a bright and healthy future for yourself and your child (optimism); increase and encourage how much your child is involved in self-improvement (achievement and activity); and monitor, model, and teach your child how to make good choices (responsibility). You live out the SOAR lifestyle yourself and then invite your child to join you in it. These are healthy, desirable goals for every human being. If you're honest, you may find you've wanted these things for yourself as well as for your child. You've just needed encouragement to reinvigorate and revitalize your goals in these areas. Don't beat yourself up for failures in the past; motivate yourself to do better in the future. You can do it!

Support—*Supporting Your Child Each Step of the Way*

Children are very sensitive to adult nuances. They interpret the moods and attitudes of the adults around them and make judgments based upon their own understanding. Sometimes those judgments are center-straight, and sometimes they are skewed by a child's misperception. That you consistently convey a positive attitude of love, acceptance, and support for your child and for these healthy changes is therefore vitally important. You must be your child's greatest advocate. All of the good you are trying to do can be undone if your child perceives there is something *wrong* or *unlovable* about him or her which is necessitating these changes. He or she receives enough negative pressure from the culture and environment without feeling deficient at home. Please remember that living a healthy life benefits everyone and should not be portrayed as a punishment for being overweight, inactive, or unhealthy.

> A healthy life isn't **punishment** for being overweight or inactive.

Optimism—*Expecting the Very Best from and for Your Child*

Your child strives to live up to your expectations. If those expectations aren't very high, your child interprets the reason as your belief that he or she is not capable. While you don't want to set the bar so high that no one could reach it, you don't want to set it so low that nothing is accomplished.

How do you maintain a balance yourself between too high and too low of expectations? By consistently presenting opportunities for positive change while praising your child for every victory, no matter how small. Each child is different and will require a different time frame. This isn't a race to see whose family can become the "healthiest" the quickest. It's about providing a nurturing, healthy environment that allows each person the opportunity to grow and change.

And remember, as you provide this environment for your child, you're also providing it for yourself. Don't be afraid to expect good things from you! As a family, you are all in it together. As a parent, you are in the driver's seat in so many ways. I encourage you to believe in yourself, believe in your child, and believe that God is with you. The family unit is of utmost concern to him. He created it, planned for it, and nurtures it with his own love and support. You are not alone! I've seen the wonderful changes families have made to restore a healthy, balanced life. It's yours for the taking. Have courage—have patience—have faith.

Active Achievement—*Promoting Physical Activity over Passive Entertainment*

One of the primary areas in which we need to encourage our child's achievement is the realm of physical activity. As parents, we need to confess that we have allowed our children to vegetate in front of television sets, game consoles, and computer screens far too much. We've congratulated them for spending five hours in front of a television screen to get to the next "level." We've used electronic babysitters for our own convenience, allowing them to consume our children's energy so we could conserve our own. This needs to stop. Your child needs to get out and play, move, exercise, and have fun physically. This is the only way he or she can achieve a healthy, active physical lifestyle.

Your child needs to get outside and play.

No pill or package can do this—only consistent physical activity and movement. You'll need to make adjustments to your own schedule and habits in order for this to happen. As much as possible, you need to spend active time with your children. As an active, vibrant person yourself, you can motivate your child to desire the same.

Responsibility—*Integrating Good Nutrition into a Fast-Food World*

Children are the best judges of when they are hungry. They are not, however, the best judges of what to eat when they are hungry. High-calorie, high-fat, high-sugar food and drink sing out a siren song to today's children. As a responsible parent, your job is not to forbid certain types of food but rather to help your child understand healthy food and nutrition. From this basis, your child can make positive food choices whether you are present or not. And as you choose what you will have available and prepare for your child, you help create a palate that appreciates healthy food and is able to withstand the constant temptation of unhealthy choices. Taking responsibility in this area will provide a wonderful model for the other, nonfood areas of growing up.

Helping Your Family to SOAR

What do you think of when you hear the word SOAR? Doesn't it conjure up feelings of lightness, exhilaration, and freedom? As parents, none of us wants our children to be weighed down with stress and worry, with excess weight and the ostracism it produces, with feelings of dread or hopelessness. Instead, we want our children to be able to soar above their trials and problems, to overcome and learn from them, to look to God for guidance and inspiration. All these things are possible, and you are the key.

I encourage you to read and work through this book carefully. You may begin to implement positive changes as you read, but you might also want to read the book in its entirety before beginning. This isn't a sprint to some fantasy, size-0 world. It's a daily walk integrating emotional, relational, physical, and spiritual principles within the SOAR concept. Take time to digest the ideas, suggestions, and steps presented. Allow them to inspire you to create your own.

Most of all, believe that with God, you have the power to provide the kind of life for your child and your family which you know will be pleasing to God. This kind of life will bless your child now and provide healthy and happy habits for the rest of his or her life. But it takes a daily commitment on your part. Let's start that daily walk together.

1

Preflight

Suppose one of you wants to build a tower. Will he not first sit down and estimate the cost to see if he has enough money to complete it?

Luke 14:28

When you picked up this book, you were looking to make a change in your family—to take a journey, if you will, from where you are right now to a healthier and hopefully happier destination. For any journey, though, you need to take stock before you leave. Likewise, before we take off and SOAR, we need to spend some time in preflight preparation. This chapter will help you to

- be sure of your departure point (understand where you and your family are right now)
- understand why you're taking this flight (assess your motivations for positive family changes)
- draw up a reasonable flight path (evaluate your goals and make sure they are appropriate and attainable)

- commit to the flight (understand your role as encourager, active participant, and role model)
- prepare passengers for the flight (engage the entire family in the positive changes)
- be alert to adverse flying conditions (honestly assess your own lifestyle choices and issues with food)
- keep in contact with air traffic control (be sure you're spiritually grounded before you take off and during the flight)

The success of SOAR, or any endeavor for that matter, can hinge upon preparation. Imagine, for example, you were asked to present a ten-minute speech on a contemporary topic. You could just go up in front of that room full of people and, based upon what you already know, talk for ten minutes. But what if you took an hour beforehand to gather some additional information, check resources, organize your thoughts on paper, and mentally go over what you'll say? Not only would you feel more confident, your talk would be of greater value to the audience, though it would last the same amount of time. When you prepare appropriately for a task, you increase the value of the outcome. I know you desire a valuable outcome for your family!

So take the time to really work through this chapter. Journal your answers honestly. Come to understand yourself, your child, and your family patterns and habits. In this way you'll anticipate potential challenges for yourself and for each member of the family. After all, change isn't easy—but as the saying goes, this change is going to do you and your family good!

Answering the "Where": Be Sure of Your Departure Point

You can't get where you're going unless you know where you are. It's time to take an honest look at your family—your situation in life right now, how each member is doing, and how you all interact together. This should include those family members who may not live in the home but maintain consistent family contact—for example, extended family caregivers or non-custodial parents.

Get out a sheet of paper or journal and list every member of the family. Leave plenty of room between each name so you can write down information and observations about each later. Don't worry about putting yourself down just yet; first I want you to concentrate on the other members of the family.

> You can't get where you're going unless you know where you are.

Now I want you to list each family member's strengths. For very young children, go ahead and mention personality traits you are aware of as well as their tender age—this is a positive in and of itself in the process of change. Before you consider the improvements you wish to make to the family, I want you to acknowledge the strengths already present. You will be able to draw out and enhance these strengths as you SOAR. Be as generous and optimistic as you can be about each person. In this way you can communicate positive expectations based on their strengths and abilities.

Also be aware of personality traits that may prove challenging as you implement changes. Later in this chapter, we'll look at ways you can meet these challenges. For now, just write down what they are. (A word of caution here: because you are giving forthright, adult evaluations, please be sure to keep this information secured from younger family members. This assessment is not meant for you to share with the entire family, though it is appropriate for you to share with the other parent or other adults.)

Next, I'd like you to think about what each family member values. What is important to him or her? For example, if each were given a choice of three things to have on a desert island, what would they choose and why? For each person, think about the first thing he or she does when he or she gets up in the morning (for younger children) or gets home at the end of the day (for older children and adults). Having a clear understanding of what motivates each family member is important. You want to concentrate on enhancing the positives as opposed to reacting against the negatives. This entails motivation through positive responses and activities, as opposed to threats of negative consequences.

> Having a clear understanding of what **motivates** each family member is important.

Now that you've assessed each person in the family, I'd like you to think of the family as a whole. What are your family's strengths? What are the areas you really excel in as a unit? When other people talk to you about your family in a positive way, what are the things they mention? As you compare your family to other families, what can you identify as areas of stability and consistency?

Now, how about challenges? Although few people will openly speak to you about these challenges, you're probably aware of what they are. These are the challenges you live with day-to-day. They're probably those things that are a source of concern and frustration. It's time to acknowledge and address them. As your family operates as a unit, where are the gaps?

Next, identify if a particular family member embodies a particular strength or challenge. For example, if your family attends religious services regularly, is that due to the efforts of one family member more than another? Or does your family find it hard to have evening meals together daily due to the schedule of a particular person? Often you can bring about positive change through working with a single family member who in turn affects all the others.

At this point, engage in a little visualization. You've probably got a pretty good idea of the types of changes you'd like to see in your family. First, envision how you think each person may react to those changes, both positive and negative. After all, forewarned is forearmed. However, be prepared to be surprised, especially the older the person. Next, envision how your family life will improve once these changes are established. That's the scene I want you to hold onto!

Answer honestly—how close are you to that future? Do you feel you're pretty far down the road and just looking to make some modifications that will help you get there faster and stay there longer? Or do you find yourself facing a wide divide between where your family is now and where you want it to be? Are you a disjointed family, with some family members who have a considerably farther way to go than others? This exercise isn't meant to discourage you! Whatever your particular situation, the joy of SOAR is that through it you have the ability to start wherever you are right now and ensure the whole family arrives together at your desired destination.

Answering the "Why": Understand Why You Want to SOAR

We've talked about the rest of the family; let's take a moment to focus on you. You are the catalyst for change. After all, if you were completely satisfied with how things were going with your family, you probably would not have bought this book. But some motivation compelled you to pick it up. You've reached that point where you're ready to take action. What I'd like you to focus on and articulate for yourself is *why*. Then when bumpy weather hits, you'll have a set of identifiable reasons you can hold onto to keep you on a steady course. It's like the difference between flying by sight and flying by instruments. You will have times when everything is going just great and your family is SOARing high. You can see that the way ahead is clear. But when the rough weather hits and clouds form around you, your internal motivation is like the correct instrument settings on a plane. Even when others can't see the progress or why changes are positive, you'll be able to guide them along the journey successfully because of your internal conviction about your reasons for change.

I don't know what all of your reasons are. Some of them will be pretty basic, much like those of many other families, and we'll certainly talk about those. But some of them will be highly personal, and that's fine. My job is to provide you with direction and encouragement so *you* can change your family.

I want you to write down three reasons for instituting these family changes. If you have trouble coming up with three, think back to what made you pick up this book in the first place. What about the content resonated with you? You might say something like, "I want our family to be a family again." Or, "I don't want my daughter to be overweight like I was." Or, "I want my son to develop self-confidence and be happy with who he is as a person." For whatever reason, you perceive that some part of your family's life and health have gone off track.

Take some time to expand upon each of your three reasons. For example, if one of yours was similar to the first—"I want our family to be a family again"—you may write down something like, "We all live such distinct, separate lives. Each of us is so busy doing our own activities that we never stop long enough just to be a family. We're always running from this event to that function, grabbing dinner on the run or in the car. By the time we get home at night, we're so tired it's all we can do to finish up chores or schoolwork and go to bed. We're not eating or doing things as a family like we should. I want us to have a family life."

Or you might write down something like this: "I don't want my daughter to be overweight like I was. I look at her and I see myself growing up. I know how it feels to be called 'fat' and be unpopular in school, but I don't know how to help her lose the weight. I don't want to make her feel even worse by telling her I think she's fat too. After all, who am I to talk about weight? And I surely don't want her to develop an eating disorder. I just keep hoping she'll outgrow the weight, but it hasn't happened yet. I want her to be a healthy weight."

Or your reason might look something like this: "I want my son to develop self-confidence and be happy with who he is as a person. He just seems so introverted, like he's never really happy. He stays inside a lot and either watches television or sits at the computer. It's like pulling teeth to get him outside to do anything, though it's not like we have a lot of time after school and work anyway. I think he'd feel better about himself if he could find something he was really good at, but it's so hard to get him to try something new. I want him to like who he is."

> At the heart of your motivation should be the welfare of those you love.

At the heart of your motivation should be the welfare of those you love. Having extrinsic, outwardly-focused motivation based upon the good of others is completely appropriate—even biblical. This is the heart of God's message to us: "For God so loved the world that he gave his one and only Son, that whoever believes in him shall not perish but have eternal life" (John 3:16). Love for us was God's motivation for taking action; following his example will help you tap into divine strength and wisdom.

Come up with short, one-phrase statements you can put to memory for each of your motivations. You can even write them down on a piece of paper and keep them handy, though private from younger eyes. These are for you; later you can help each member of the family identify their own reasons for wanting to SOAR.

Answering the "Where": Draw Up a Reasonable Flight Path

As you consider where you want to go, remember, SOAR isn't about having the "perfect" family or accomplishing the goal in the shortest amount of time possible. This sets the family up for unrealistic expectations, which, like ice on a wing, can bring a plane down faster than just about anything. Instead, you need to strive for a destination built on realistic expectations and create an appropriate time frame to arrive.

In order to do this, we're going to take a look at your motivations, factor in the realities of where your family is right now, and create achievable goals. Let's continue with the three sample motivations already introduced. For the first one, "I want our family to be a family again," one could be tempted to dream of a destination that has more in common with a family in the 1950s than with the realities of twenty-first-century American life. Part of you may wistfully contemplate a goal of family sit-down meals every day of the week—with all members present and fresh, healthy, homemade food eaten in an unhurried atmosphere of mutual love and respect. For a small portion of you, this could be a realistic reality, given your personal situation. However, many households today have both parents working, children in a day care situation, planned activities in the evenings, and a constant time pressure to get everything done. While it is possible to evaluate your situation and make positive changes—and you will—it's not realistic to set ideals that would require a change back to the days of *Ozzie and Harriet*. The older your children are, the more activities the family can be involved in and the greater the challenge to provide the logistics where the members can all come together.

A reasonable goal in your situation may be sitting down to dinner at least four nights a week, though not always on the same night each week. Be realistic; you don't want to cascade down into defeatism and determine nothing can positively change. Remember, you do have control over your family's schedule and priorities. You can make four nights a week an obtainable goal. You might start with two nights as a minimum and work up from there. Hopefully, as your family sees the benefit from these shared meals together, each member will make them a personal priority.

Let's take a look at the next example—"I don't want my daughter to be overweight like I was." Your goal may be for your child to finally break the cycle of family obesity. But you may envision that goal making her thin and popular, perhaps like you were not. It's important to remember that high school includes few sports stars and cheerleaders and only one homecoming queen. If your secret destination for your family is to produce such a luminary, it makes every other destination a wrong turn. That's not fair.

> **Remember, you do have control over your family's schedule and priorities.**

Because your motivation is twofold, having to do with your child and with yourself, you need to guard against tying your child's success onto your own personal pain. If you were overweight as a child or are overweight now, these realities cannot be ameliorated by your child achieving a healthy weight. In other words, you need to avoid the temptation to rewrite your past through your child's future. This can be a fairly common temptation for parents, and not just in dealing with weight.

A companion temptation for parents is to pressure their children not by trying to *rewrite* your past in their present but by trying to *relive* your past in their present. Perhaps you were the sports star or the academic whiz kid or the prom queen. If so, you cannot realistically insist that your child duplicate the same success. Your desired destination for your child or your family cannot be calculated from this viewpoint. Again, you are setting up unrealistic expectations that will weigh your child and your family down.

Your child is his or her own person, with a personal destiny given by God. Their goal is to follow in Christ's footsteps, not yours. Realize the path your child takes to success—even their definition of success—may be completely different from yours. As long as you both keep Christ as your focus, you're both heading in the same direction. Trust God to make sure each of you arrives.

In order to keep yourself firmly grounded, your goal for your daughter should be to attain an age and body-type appropriate weight over time. Deep down health, not surface appearances, should be the motivating factor. This will instill a respect for her body that can extend over a variety of areas.

You also may be tempted, once a challenge has been admitted to and a solution seized upon, to want to "fix" things quickly. Let's look at this in light of the third example—"I want my son to have self-confidence and be happy with who he is as a person." You may decide that it's normal for kids to be happy, so once you start on this path, his happiness should materialize overnight. The process, however, is not as methodical as a mathematical formula. Often a child's lack of self-confidence is an outside manifestation of a multi-layered condition. Helping your child to SOAR will provide your child with the building blocks to reestablish self-confidence and self-esteem, but you cannot be in charge of how long that takes. Your job is to continue to provide the support, foundation, tools, and encouragement. The goal is progress, not perfection. On this journey toward a positive sense of self, don't shortchange your child by wanting to leapfrog over lessons in order to get to the finish line quicker. Allow your child to learn, grow, and accept himself

> God is so patient with us; be patient with your child.

at the pace needed to really set these lessons deep in his heart. God is so patient with us; be patient with your child.

You can see the importance of being clear on where you need to go. Notice I didn't say where you *want* to go. Your destination must be determined based upon family need, not your personal wants. In this way it can be embraced by the entire family, not viewed as a personal crusade. SOAR should come to permeate your family. Then it will be infused in each member even when outside of your direct sphere of influence.

Answering the "How": Commit to the Flight

Some have said that the true test of a family is the summer vacation. Sibling bickering, parental disagreements, travel stress, unfamiliar extended family, close quarters, upset schedules, and a constant "Are we there yet?" can provide abundant opportunity for people to act their worst. How each family member reacts to his or her own and everyone else's "worst" is a living testimony to the strength of family bonds. Usually someone in the family has to make it his or her job to remind everyone else of the fun you'll have, the places you'll see, the adventures you'll take, the surprises in store. This person is the vision bearer, who constantly points the way to the fun and reward. In this SOAR adventure, that's going to be your job.

In order to accomplish this task, you'll need to commit to three things: maintaining your role as family encourager; keeping yourself an active participant as a pilot, not a passenger; and accepting your position as role model for the others. This is no small responsibility, but it makes sense for you to take it on: the person who sees the challenge is usually the best suited to address it.

This isn't to say that you should go it alone and not ask for help. On the contrary, you're the conductor, but no one expects you to play all the instruments. You've already got a team in place—your family. We'll talk more about engaging their help in the next section. For now, though, let's focus on your part as the SOAR vision bearer.

You are the SOAR vision bearer.

Your first role is to be the encourager of the family. After all, you understand each person and what is important to them. You see why setting this course is important, and you are able to visualize the positive destination. At first, you'll probably need to do quite a bit of encouraging. However, I think you'll find that as time goes on your family will begin to encourage you back in ways large and small. So take courage and keep at it.

Remember to always remain an active participant. You are the pilot, even if you have a copilot. You've got to be actively involved yourself, providing creative solutions and keeping your family on track. You may need to divert your time, attention, and energy from other responsibilities to this one. Your family will need to see that you are firmly engaged in this adventure in order to relax and feel secure through the changes. How would you feel if, during a turbulent plane flight, you looked into the cockpit and saw the pilot lounging sideways in his seat, doing a crossword puzzle? Your immediate reaction would be, *Why isn't the pilot concentrating on flying the plane?* When you step into an airplane, you expect the pilot to be an active participant in the flight at all times. Your family will expect no less.

The SOAR concept cannot be accomplished by a "do as I say, not as I do" mentality. To succeed, you must accept that you will be a role model for the rest of the family. If you seek to implement the healthy changes in your family but then pick and choose which ones you're going to apply to yourself, this plane will take a nosedive. This is perhaps the most personally challenging aspect to your role as pilot—making sure you keep yourself on course because others are watching you. Now, instead of finding this an intimidating prospect, I'm asking you to *embrace* it. This is your chance to show your family, through your actions and not just your words, how important they are to you, how dedicated you are to them, and how much you love them. Through your personal faithfulness to SOAR, you'll demonstrate your level of commitment to them. Believe me, they will notice.

Answering the "Who": Prepare Passengers for the Flight

Family life ebbs and flows like the ocean, and each member of the family is like a planetary body affecting that tide. The ocean is affected by the circuits of the moon, whose gravitational pull creates the tides. Each family situation will generally include a single family member whose "gravitational pull" is greater than the others. For example, in some families, one of the children is advanced at some sort of activity—sports, music, academics, or something else. The "pull" of getting that child to practices, events, and programs affects every member of the family. You will want to be aware if a family member seems to be pulled by others more than pulling him or herself. Often this person can feel "lost" or "left out," always on the sidelines watching but rarely stepping onto the family center stage. This person may need extra attention and motivation to SOAR.

> Look for family members who have the greatest influence or impact on the others.

Likewise, you may find that one family member is adverse to change, especially the sorts of dietary changes you'll want to implement for a healthier family. This person is like the boulder at the water's edge—the tide goes in and out around it, but it does not move. How you approach this person will depend upon whether he or she is a child or an adult. Often children seem highly resistant to change. They can set their heels, drag their feet, and refuse to move forward. As the parent, however, your tide is strong enough to overcome this reluctance through patience, perseverance, and a constant forward motion.

If this person is another adult in the family, your task is going to be a bit more challenging. I recommend first having a private, heartfelt talk with that person. Remembering the motivations and reasons you've already uncovered and articulated in this chapter, go to that person and explain why you feel so strongly about wanting the family to SOAR. Put forth your personal commitment to doing what's necessary and to being a role model. Talk about the positive future you envision for the family, and attempt to engage him or her as a copilot on the journey. Offer to go through this book together or to talk with him or her regarding what you're learning in the book on a regular basis. If you're not able to obtain a copilot for your trip, try to settle for a willing passenger.

For those older family members who seem more reluctant to go along, the best course of action may be to implement the changes with as little fanfare as possible. A low-key, business-as-*mostly*-usual approach may be best.

> Big changes are less likely to set off warning bells if made in **small chunks** over time.

Big changes are less likely to set off any adolescent warning bells if they are implemented in small chunks over time. As we go into each aspect of SOAR, we'll talk specifically about how to deal with children of different ages. Initially, your goal is simply to get everybody on board.

Go back to your list of family members, including caregivers or non-custodial parents. Write down any objections you anticipate being raised by each. Now, knowing what you do about each individual, provide at least two positive responses to each of those objections. For example, a non-custodial parent may object, thinking you're going to drop off your child with detailed meal plans that must be followed to the letter. Instead, you can reassure the person by passing along some of the healthy guidelines presented in this book. Or if you know this person enjoys a special restaurant or treat with your child, assure the person that occasional treats are perfectly acceptable within an overall commitment to healthy eating.

You may face a member of your family who feels he or she doesn't have a "problem" and objects to being lumped in with the rest of the family. You can remind this person that you're not addressing a "problem" but renewing a commitment to establish a healthier lifestyle for everyone. By emphasizing the familial nature of SOAR, you can help this individual to recommit to positively engaging with other family members.

The bottom line is that not everyone in the family may initially be enthusiastic. Don't let this deter you! Anticipate the objections and proactively create positive, optimistic—but determined—responses. This isn't the time for arguments or recriminations; it's a time to bring the family together in a shared goal of companionship, mutual respect, and support.

Answering the "Through What": Be Alert to Adverse Flying Conditions

One of the first things a pilot does before taking off is to become aware of any adverse flying conditions—from a peculiarity in the design of the plane to potential thunderstorms ahead. The pilot understands that a lot can happen between the time he or she taxis to takeoff and puts wheels down to land. While not every situation can be anticipated, it's always a good idea to be aware of potential turbulence.

You can have a bumpy start, for example, if you've tried to "fix" your family before. Depending upon the method you chose and how successful it was, you may find yourself in for a bumpy start to SOAR if you encounter family resistance based upon past experience. If this is the fifth "change" you've attempted to implement in the last three years, your family may not have gotten over the last one or two . . . or three. They could be saying *Not again*.

> **Your start can be bumpy if you've tried to "fix" your family before.**

Write down in your journal what ways you've tried in the past to implement the positive changes you desire. Have you always been the person to implement these changes? What did you do? How many family members became involved? Was the reaction positive, negative, or both? How long did the changes last? Can you build on any past changes? What have you learned from past attempts that will help you now?

If this is the first such journey for your family, how your family will react remains to be seen. Be positive, optimistic, and engaged yourself, and expect the best. Be open about your own issues and your desire to do what's right for the family. Avoid the pitfall of a self-righteous attitude. Put yourself, like the apostle Paul, forward as chief among sinners and convey your enthusiasm for the future.

You'll also want to look into that future and determine if certain times and circumstances may create adverse flying conditions for one member or the whole family. For example, if you'll be taking a vacation among extended family that has not chosen to embrace a healthy lifestyle, you'll need to plot out ways around this obstacle. You might decide to bring along some food of your own, offer to cook for everyone for several days while you're there, or call ahead and explain your goals and commitment. Or you may know that your family is going to interact with a person who does not give them the respect they deserve. You've probably already tried to work with this person to alter his or her behavior. The fact that this person is still involved in the life of your family indicates a level of inevitability. Therefore, you'll need to make special preparations to minimize the contact and fortify your family members to weather the "storm" this person creates.

> **Your ultimate goal is to strengthen and mature each member of the family.**

Is a time coming when you will not have primary responsibility over all or part of your family? If so, you'll need to start early to prepare another adult or even your child to act as copilot during your absence. Remember, these are life skills you're teaching and modeling. At some point, each family member will be ready to take off and SOAR on their own. This should be your ultimate goal—the strengthening and maturing of each member of the family. The Bible is quite clear that we don't even know what's going to happen tomorrow. Help your family to SOAR by equipping them to steer a clear path whether or not you're there.

Answering the "Through Whom": Keep in Contact with the Controller

Pilots fly the plane, but they do not do so alone. Unseen are scores of air traffic controllers who track their progress, give directions, provide necessary updates, and carefully guide the plane from point A to point B. The pilot sees what's outside the cockpit window. The air traffic controller sees the big picture and can inform the pilot of unseen hazards.

Please realize you are not alone on your journey. Just as a pilot is in constant contact with the controllers, you must stay in constant contact with the Controller. God is able to guide and direct your paths. In fact, God does his own "preflight." Psalm 85:13 says that "righteousness goes before him and prepares the way for his steps." Your job is to take the way God has prepared for you and your family so you can echo Psalm 17:5, "My steps have held to your paths; my feet have not slipped."

God wants you to know you're not alone in this.

As the creator of the family, God is intimately involved with and concerned about yours. Do you consider a healthy, happy family to be a wonderful gift for all involved? James 1:17 says that "Every good and perfect gift is from above, coming down from the Father of the heavenly lights, who does not change like shifting shadows." The family is God's gift to us. When it has gone off track, his good and perfect will is to bring it back within the paths he has established. So embark on your journey with full confidence that God supports your efforts and wants you to keep in constant contact with him for direction, guidance, and help. You're not in this alone!

Now, we all know that life can get busy. Our hectic schedules leave us little time for reflection, for healthy meals, and often even for prayer and meditation. To help you stay in contact with your Controller, I want you to commit to daily prayer and meditation during this time of SOAR-ing. Each day write out your prayers to God about your family, your goals, your desires, and your challenges. And write down the answers, because he will answer you. I also want you to take time to meditate on his Word during this time. I recommend working through Psalms and Proverbs, which are full of wisdom about God, his steadfast love and constant presence, his commitment to his people, and how to live. As you seek to help yourself and your family grow in healthy life skills, this wisdom will prove invaluable.

Be open also to where God leads you as you study and pray. Listen to what your heart and other people tell you. Be open to the guidance of his Spirit, confirmed in the Word. This is a journey for your family and a spiritual journey for you. His strength will sustain you when yours fails. His wisdom will provide answers when you have none. His direction will shine when the way seems dark. His patience will endure when yours has given out. His love will uphold you always.

If you have not already written down your thoughts, feelings, and reflections as directed in this chapter, I strongly encourage you to go back and do so. Take the time you need to be clear in your mind about each aspect of this preflight preparation. If you've already written down your thoughts, take this opportunity to go back and refresh what you've done.

With our preflight completed, we're ready to take off and SOAR, right after we check in with air traffic control:

Father, thank you for helping me understand my family. I'm ready to take flight for the good of my family. Grant me the vision to see progress each day. I will need your guidance, wisdom, strength, and encouragement. Help me to know you are with me. I accept that you have placed this desire—your desire— for my family's good on my heart. Help me to love my family by being faithful to this call. Amen.

2

S Is for Support

Better a meal of vegetables where there is love than a fattened calf with hatred.

Proverbs 15:17

How do you help someone? What form does support take? How do you know if what you're offering is really what the other person needs? Even if it's needed, how do you know if this is the right time to offer it? Saying you will offer support is one thing; having that support accepted and utilized is another. The support you provide for SOAR must be both accepted by your family and utilized by each member. Therefore we need to consider the kind of support you'll be giving and how to offer that support in order to have the highest chance of it being accepted and utilized.

A healthy life through SOAR is of benefit to everyone and is not meant as a punishment for being overweight, inactive, or unhealthy. How your support is packaged is important. If it is wrapped in condemnation, frustration, disappointment, or criticism, it's no gift. Your child and your family need to integrate healthy habits, behaviors, and lifestyle; these are good things. You don't want to package these good things so they appear bad and are rejected. Listen to Luke 11:11–12: "Which of you fathers, if your son asks for a fish, will give him a snake instead? Or if he asks for an egg, will give him a scorpion?" You're probably thinking, *If my child asked for an egg, of course I wouldn't give him a scorpion!* Two perspectives, however, should be considered—yours and your child's. Unfortunately, in our desperation for change and frustration over past failures, we can cloak our good intentions—our fish—in critical, demanding camouflage that causes them to look more like snakes. Is it any wonder, then, that our good intentions are rebuffed? This only makes us more critical and frustrated. We think, *What's wrong with that person? Why did he turn down my fish? The way he reacted, you'd think I'd tried to give him a snake!*

> To be **effective**, support must be accepted and utilized.

Motivating your family to accept positive, healthy changes is no different. You've already determined that your family needs these fish and eggs; make sure you don't present them as snakes and scorpions! Support for SOAR needs to come through the positive components of stability, love, and acceptance, not through desperation, criticism, and frustration.

> If your support is wrapped in negativity, it's no gift.

Take a moment to think about your pattern for providing direction and instruction to your family. How do you frame your comments? Are they focused on negative behavior? Or are they focused on reiterating the positive characteristics you believe about the other person? What is your pattern of motivation? Do you tend to raise your voice or vent your frustration? In order for you to provide your family with stability, love, and acceptance, you must ask God to help you grow in those areas yourself. If you have developed a negative pattern of criticism, sarcasm, frustration, or anger in motivating and instructing family members, you'll need to intentionally change in order to SOAR.

Verbal Support

The words you use are vital to the SOAR concept. In fact, the words you use are vital in all areas of your relationship with your family. Consider these three Scripture verses:

Pleasant words promote instruction.

Proverbs 16:21

Pleasant words are a honeycomb, sweet to the soul and healing to the bones.

Proverbs 16:24

A man of knowledge uses words with restraint, and a man of understanding is even-tempered.

Proverbs 17:27

Do you see the importance of the words you use to communicate SOAR concepts and your demeanor while presenting them? You want your attitude and your words to be pleasant, not critical, and your demeanor to be even-tempered, not frustrated.

Now, you may ask, *Why all this focus on my words? What does it matter what I say, as long as I tell the truth?* The answer is found in Job 6:25, which says, "How painful are honest words! But what do your arguments prove?" When family members are resistant to positive changes, confronting them with the truth about their negative behavior and your positive changes may be necessary. But, as Job says, it's important to be aware of what your arguments will prove. You don't want to win your argument by crushing or belittling your opponent, especially if that "opponent" is a reluctant child or reticent spouse. SOAR is not meant to be coercive, nor is it meant to give you "ammunition" to blast your family for past mistakes or behaviors.

Be a healer to your family through the wise words you choose.

Your family will listen to what you say *and* how you say it to determine its validity and how to respond. Your words will be either your greatest ally or your greatest enemy in motivating your family. "Reckless words pierce like a sword, but the tongue of the wise brings healing" (Prov. 12:18). Be a healer to your family through the wise words you choose.

Support by Example

Remember, SOAR requires your personal commitment. Yes, it's very much about what you say, but it's also very much about what you do. Your words must be supported by your own positive actions and attitude. If your pattern of instructing your family involves *telling* them what to do out of frustration instead of *modeling* what to do through positive example, you're apt to encounter resistance. In contrast, when your family sees you "walking the talk," you will demonstrate not only your commitment but also *equity*. People see a fundamental unfairness in the "do as I say, not as I do" pattern of instruction. However, tremendous bonding can occur through "we're all in it together" actions.

You want your actions and your words to complement, not compete against, each other. Think about the concept taught in James 2:22: "You see that his faith and his actions were working together, and his faith was made complete by what he did." Now, insert "words" in the place of faith and here's what you get: "You see that his words and his actions were working together, and his words were made complete by what he did." This is how you are to integrate your words and your actions for the benefit of your family!

Providing Stability

Remember, we said that the support you provide for your family to SOAR needs to come through stability, love, and acceptance. Let's look at the first aspect, *stability*, by going back to our flying analogy for a moment. I don't know about you, but when I fly, I like to know the pilot will keep the plane steady and stable. I don't want any loop-de-loops, corkscrew turns, vertical climbs, or stalling dives. My stomach just couldn't take it! I feel better when I know that my flight will be as smooth as possible and the pilot is in control, taking my comfort to heart.

As you embark on your SOAR journey, realize your family feels exactly like I do. They need to know that you are prepared to provide a journey toward a healthier lifestyle that is as stable as possible. How do you provide stability? Through maintaining consistency. Now, this doesn't mean being consistently critical or consistently angry. I'm talking about presenting yourself and the specific SOAR changes in a consistently positive and upbeat way. It also means not wavering in your commitment and your decision to provide your family with the good things it needs to be healthy and happy.

> **Stability** is achieved through positive consistency.

One way to help you maintain this consistency is to visualize these changes as permanent, not as a response to specific events or situations. In other words, these changes are to become part of the fabric of your family. Say, for example, your family needed to move to a different town.

This is a major change; it isn't a trip or a vacation, and you wouldn't present it that way. In order to help your family with the transition, you would present the move as permanent and in as positive a manner as possible. Change can be unsettling, and your consistency and optimism provide a steadiness for everyone else. Your family is *moving* toward a healthier, happier life together. You must present it as a natural, permanent part of the family, not a transitory, temporary situation that will go away if they just present enough resistance to your latest "cause." Besides, moving can be fun! It's a chance to clean out, reevaluate, and discover new friends and adventures. All of these things you'll do through SOAR: you'll be cleaning out unhealthy habits, reevaluating your current lifestyle, discovering new "friends" in healthy patterns, and engaging in the family adventure called life.

Back to the plane again—what happens if it hits a great deal of turbulence and instability during a flight? Besides everybody feeling pretty lousy, you're trapped in your seats. The captain won't turn off the "fasten seat belt" sign. Your movement is restricted because you don't know when the next drop will happen; even getting up to go to the bathroom becomes chancy. A stable ride means people are free to move about the cabin and enjoy the flight. If you provide an emotionally bumpy ride or an inconsistent roller coaster of commitment, your family will hunker down in their seats just waiting for the flight to be over. Stability allows your family to weather the initial "takeoff" of SOAR and relax and enjoy the ride!

Providing stability helps your family relax and enjoy the ride!

As you seek to provide stability to your family, consider God's example of stability, often called in Scripture being *steadfast*. One of my favorite passages on this is Lamentations 3:22–23: "The steadfast love of the LORD never ceases, his mercies never come to an end; they are new every morning; great is your faithfulness" (NRSV). This is the heart of stability—God's steadfast love for us. And we can be assured of his love because, as James tells us, "Every good and perfect gift is from above, coming down from the Father of the heavenly lights, who does not change like shifting shadows" (James 1:17). If we know and believe that God desires good and perfect things for our families, then be assured that God will provide you what you need to support these good and perfect things. He will not change his support or his mind; do not change yours.

Love

As you present your family with the need for change, make sure your support is firmly wrapped in love. This love may seem like a given, but again, it's important to be aware of perspective. Your love can seem like a scorpion if it comes with the sting of conditionality. You don't want your family to take your desire for change as dissatisfaction with who they are as individuals. If they felt they could only win your love by losing weight, becoming popular, performing better in school, or accomplishing any number of positive changes, that would be tragic. Your love needs to be like God's love—unconditional, unwavering, and motivational, yet supportive at all times.

> Like God, don't emphasize the outside, but instead focus on the inside.

Again, this goes back to your personal motivation. If your family perceives that you're doing this so everyone in the family will be thin, look healthy, or perform well in sports or school, this could be construed as you concentrating on the external, not the internal. God fixes his sights on our insides, knowing that when our hearts are happy and strong, the outward things tend to fall into place on their own. First Samuel 16:7 says, "The Lord does not look at the things man looks at. Man looks at the outward appearance, but the LORD looks at the heart."

I'd like you to get your journal and draw a large heart for each family member. Write down what you see in each one's heart. What are they made of? What words capture their essence? Now, how can your love combine with their hearts to produce the best possible response to and outcome from these changes? How can you best communicate your love? Will one family member need extra space to come on board on their own? Will another need extra coaching to understand the need for these changes? Will yet another need to operate as a "copilot" in order to accept and honor the changes? Know each member of your family and be prepared to modify your approach to reach them.

Love is a powerful emotion manifested in many different ways. In motivating your family to SOAR, you'll need to be like the description of God in Psalm 62:11–12: "One thing God has spoken, two things have I heard: that you, O God, are strong, and that you, O Lord, are loving. Surely you will reward each person according to what he has done." God knows each one of us; we are individuals to him. The stability you provide through consistency doesn't mean a lockstep approach to each person. The desired results are universal, but the way you lovingly encourage and support each person will require flexibility and creativity. Instead of viewing this as a lot more work on your part, think of this as a way to really get to know and understand these people you love.

How do you show this love? Memorize 1 Corinthians 13 so you'll have these love attributes in your memory to call up as different situations arise. As you prepare yourself to support your family, I'd like you to personalize this passage of Scripture and write it in your journal. Be specific and envision this as your commitment to love throughout the process. Be detailed and think about your own shortcomings and how this commitment can help you to be aware of them and overcome them. You might write something like this:

> As I help my family to SOAR, I will be patient with each person. I will be kind in word and action. I will not envy the success of others. I will not boast in my own success. I will not be prideful of the positive changes my family is undergoing. I will not be rude when I speak or correct other members of my family. I will remember that these changes are for the good of the family, not so I can look better as a parent. I will intentionally hold my anger, and I refuse to become the family historian of every slipup or backward step along the way. I won't say "I told you so" if someone falters but will always be the family encourager. I will protect the honor of my family, especially when I speak to others outside of the family. I will trust my family to do what is right. I will always hope for the very best. Though it may get rough at times, I'm in this for the duration because my family is worth the effort. With God's help, wisdom, and strength, I won't fail my family.

Acceptance

I've touched on this point before: your family must feel your acceptance of them right where they are today. Be alert to any member of the family feeling as if there is something wrong with him or her and that this "wrongness" is the reason for these changes. You may need to do some additional supportive work with that family member before you start. Any time a change highlights a weakness or perceived weakness in one family member, you'll need to take steps to reiterate your love and acceptance. You'll also need to work with other family members to make sure they do the same.

Let's say, for example, you have a child with a history of being overweight. As soon as you make dietary changes

> **Be prepared to provide additional support to struggling family members.**

that modify the level of fats and sugars, overall calories, or even portion sizes in the food your family is provided, the overweight child could become a target of reaction by other family members who liked the "old system." You'll need to present these changes as beneficial for *everyone*, yourself included, and not just as a way to target a single person's weight. Eating healthy is not a "reaction" to someone's weight. Rather, it's part of a vibrant, healthy lifestyle for your family. It's about not deprivation but bountifully giving your body what God designed for it to use for fuel.

Or perhaps one child is an underachiever. This can be especially challenging in a family if another family member excels in one or more areas in life. As soon as you begin to address the idea of achievement and activity, the underachiever will know that finger is pointing dead center. The child who excels may feel any changes are personally unnecessary. However, all of us can be reminded of the good things God has planned for our lives and the blessing of discovering that purpose and aiming for it. Even small children have a God-given purpose. Read Ephesians 2:10 and ask yourself if this verse mentions any exceptions: "For we are God's workmanship, created in Christ Jesus to do good works, which God prepared in advance for us to do." Even highly capable people need to be reminded that God has a purpose for their life and is the author of any gifts they possess. Jeremiah 29:11 reminds us that God has a plan for each of us: "'For I know the plans I have for you,' declares the LORD, 'plans to prosper you and not to harm you, plans to give you hope and a future.'" Our desire to achieve and be active is not to produce self-congratulations. Rather, it is in order to be engaged in this future God has provided, being alert to the hope promised and ready to respond to those good works.

God accepts us right where we are today. His love compels him to make plans to prosper us in the future. In the same way, show your acceptance of each member of your family today, and let them know your love for them and their bright future is the motivation for these changes, not a perceived deficiency in any member of the family.

Support Scenarios

As you think about the best way to support your family through these changes, you will need to determine how best to respond and react within your own family. However, over the course of my counseling practice, I've seen some examples of what not to do, and I will pass these along so you can be aware of them.

Mood Motivator

The first is what I call the Mood Motivator. This person is willing to do what it takes to support a program or changes only when in the mood. If it becomes a little difficult, if resistance comes, if tired or simply not in the mood, he or she gives in and falls back to old habits. The family, aware of this pattern, may respond in a neutral way to what this person proposes initially, certain that eventually his or her mood will shift and everything will settle down, back to normal. The Mood Motivator is generally a person who jumps from idea to idea, hoping to find just the right one that will accomplish the goal without much work or effort on his or her part.

Born-Again Bully

The second type I've termed the Born-Again Bully. This is a person who determines that changes need to be made and is determined to force compliance in all areas by all members of the family through whatever means are necessary. Generally their motivation is the "good" of the family, but they tend to go about accomplishing this good in very destructive ways. Tragically, any good is decimated by the negative by-products of their rigid, usually self-righteous stance. Often this person will have undergone some sort of positive change and is zealously trying to re-create that success in their loved ones. Hyper-vigilant, this person watches all conduct and makes pointed, negative comments regarding what is happening with each member of the family, often contrasting that behavior with their own personal testimonial about the changes. While their words may have an element of truth in them, generally they end up doing more to stroke a streak of self-righteous ego than to create any lasting motivation for positive change in others.

Seesaw Supporter

The third type of person is a Seesaw Supporter. Do you remember the playground seesaws of years ago? It was essentially a flat, broad piece of wood balanced over a base in the middle. One child would climb onto each end, and by pushing off with their feet, they could cause each other to go up and down alternately. While this up-and-down motion is great fun to a child on a playground, it leaves much to be desired when applied to supporting a family for positive change. A Seesaw Supporter waxes and wanes in his or her support of those changes. One day he's fired up, enthusiastic about the changes. The next day that enthusiasm has dropped like a rock and is barely able to get off the ground. A few days later up it pops again, and everyone is supposed to climb on board with renewed enthusiasm. All of that up-and-down, on-again, off-again movement just tends to alienate the family. They'd rather just get off the ride altogether.

Can you see how each of these has an inherent flaw? The first relies on an initial burst of motivation but has no staying power over the long haul. The second certainly has staying power, but the hot blast of personal convictions burns out the rest of the family. The last ends up taking the family exactly where a real seesaw does—nowhere.

What kind of supporter do you want to be for your family? What would you term how you have acted in the past? How can you best implement these changes and motivate your family to accept and integrate them? Take some time to list out your challenges and your strengths. Write a positive scenario that addresses how you're going to encourage and guide your family. It might go something along these lines:

> I'm going to be a Tortoise Supporter. Just like the story of the rabbit and the turtle, I'm going to remember that "slow and steady wins the race." I'm not going to be jumpy and jerky like the rabbit but focused and measured like the tortoise. This will give me time to pray, plan, and think about my own actions each step of the way. I recognize that in order to develop life skills and positive habits, I need to think of this as a long-distance race, not a sprint. Instead of trying to get to the finish line the fastest, I'm going to take the time to really get to know myself and my family. I'm not interested in being first if my family doesn't make it to the finish line with me. I will allow God to cover me and my efforts, like a shell, for strength and protection.

I applaud you for reading this and taking the time to think about the content and character of the support and encouragement you are about to give. I hope you've taken the time to write down the suggestions in your journal. If you haven't done so yet, I urge you to as you finish this chapter. You don't need to race through this book. Rather, take your time and think about the concepts and ideas presented. Visualize yourself in different situations as you support your family collectively and each member individually. Think about the strength of your own motivation and pinpoint those areas where you will need to spend time in prayer asking God for strength, wisdom, and guidance.

I really want you to think about this idea of support, even before we go into the rest of the "nuts and bolts" of the SOAR plan. Why? Because especially in dealing with children, the type of support you give will determine whether or not they integrate the elements of SOAR. Not just what you offer but how you offer it makes all the difference to your family.

> **Not just what you offer but how you offer it makes all the difference to your family.**

These positive, healthy changes can be made with everyone still speaking to each other! By making this a family adventure, you can bring those fringe members closer to the core. Is the SOAR plan about a healthy weight and an optimistic attitude, an active lifestyle and an acceptance of personal responsibility? Absolutely! But it's also about bringing your family together and fortifying mutual love, acceptance, and respect.

As you model this support to each family member, you communicate the value and importance you put on each person and on the family as a whole. And you encourage each member to view each other member in the same way. If one issue you face is that each family member does not honor and respect the other, SOAR will help reestablish the healthy relationships vital for a loving, connected family.

Finding Your Own Support

On this flight, your own way is bound to hit a bumpy patch or stall out for a bit. When that happens, please know that God is the best source for personal support. Other members of the family may also encourage you along the way. If you have a copilot who is as committed to SOAR as you are, that's just great! As the SOAR vision bearer, yours is the hand that holds the wheel. But your hand may become tired and falter. When that happens, remember the story of the battle of Joshua against the Amalekites, told in Exodus 17:8–14. Joshua was sent out to do battle against the enemies of Israel, but it was Moses's job to stand on a hillside and hold up the staff of God in his hand. As long as Moses held the staff up high, Israel prevailed. Whenever Moses would falter and drop his hand, the Amalekites took the "upper hand" in the battle.

Moses, Joshua, and the nation of Israel had a dilemma—Moses needed support! So what was the answer? You might think it was to pray to God that Moses would remain strong and could hold his hand up until Israel was victorious. And that's not a bad answer; it just isn't the right one for this instance. Instead, God sent Aaron and Hur to come alongside Moses, provide him with a rock so he had a place to sit down, and then literally stand on each side of him and support Moses's outstretched hands. And Joshua's army overwhelmed the enemy.

God's support for you can come in a variety of ways. Certainly Moses was praying and talking to God all through the battle, which you will need to do also. God also brought people to Moses's side to support him during the battle. Notice that Aaron and Hur did not take the staff of God from Moses's hand. In the same way, you may not have anyone else you can "hand off" responsibility to. But you can pray that God will send you supporters, people who will encourage you and help share your load. And God himself will also be there to support you and uphold you in this battle for the well being of your family.

> **Pray that God will send you people to encourage you and share your load.**

Moses knew and understood that he was part of God's plan for victory. He trusted God to provide him with the support he needed to do what God had called him to do. He accepted the form that help came in, and Joshua prevailed in battle. And notice this: the battle itself wasn't Moses's; Joshua was the one commanding the army. In this battle for your family, you have your part to play, but the battle belongs to the Lord. The changes you want to integrate into your family are based on God's wisdom for what each person needs to grow up strong, to prosper, and to have a healthy and happy life.

Before we leave this chapter on support, I'd like you to take a moment and ask God for strength, wisdom, and guidance in this area.

Father, I recognize how important my support is to my family. I really want us to live a healthier, happier life, using your guiding principles. Give me the strength, wisdom, and guidance I need to help win this battle. I trust you to supply me with the support and help I need to be able to support my family. Show me areas of my life that might hinder me. Show me attitudes and behaviors that are contrary to your example of loving support. Keep me close to you during this time. Help me to remember the love you have for each member of my family and to love them as you do. Amen.

3

O Is for Optimism

"For I know the plans I have for you," declares the LORD, "plans to prosper you and not to harm you, plans to give you hope and a future."

Jeremiah 29:11

Of all the support you provide your family, nothing is more important than the vision of a positive future. This vision has been called a number of things—faith, hope, belief. I'm going to call this vision *optimism*, for it is the *O* in SOAR. This optimism has its roots in God's love and blessing. From these roots spring the joined stalks of positive and patient anticipation. From these stalks blossom a belief in your child's success and future.

Think of this optimism as your horizon line, to use our flight analogy. Knowing your horizon line is absolutely vital to the safety and success of your flight. This line helps you to know what is sky and what is land or water. Knowing this would seem simple, but in a turbulent storm or the black of night or even in the monotony of certain landscapes, this horizon line can become confused. Pilots flying without instruments have tragically crashed into the earth, believing instead they were climbing into the sky. Their vision was turned upside down because they lost their true horizon. As you help your family, especially your children, to SOAR, you don't want this to happen. Families who lose their horizon line of a positive future for all members can crash, just like planes.

> Nothing is more important than your belief in a **positive future** for your family.

The Horizon Line of Empty or Full

Over my years of counseling individuals and families, I've seen what happens when this horizon line of optimism becomes lost. The long-term damage it creates can extend for decades. What obscures optimism in a family? Well, I've seen perfectionism, pessimism, pride, apathy, fear, guilt, anger, blame, and shame all obliterate the family's ability to believe in each other. Allow me to share an example of what I mean.

Brad came to work with us at The Center as a young man in his twenties. He was struggling with self-esteem issues that translated into a dependence upon alcohol. Unable to hold a job, he continued to live at home, making constant demands upon his parents. These demands drained their emotional and financial resources and alienated him from the rest of his siblings. Everyone in the family, including extended family living nearby, seemed to have tried to help Brad but was burned in the process. Many family members had already given up on him, deeming him beyond help and not worth another chance. Others saw our mental health and chemical dependency treatment agency as his last chance.

We were able to address and treat Brad's reliance upon alcohol as well as work with him to uncover the roots of his addiction. Brad's answers and demeanor began to reveal that his drinking was fueled not by an attraction to alcohol but by repulsion from something else. Brad had turned to alcohol due to some pain he was attempting to self-medicate and numb. As we worked with him to dig deeper, we helped him discover how and when his world had turned upside down and he had lost his horizon line of hope.

> **Brad and his parents had lost their horizon line of hope.**

Most people know the half empty/half full glass analogy. It goes something like this: when people look at a glass containing liquid up to the middle, some will see the glass as half empty and some will see the glass as half full. Those who see it as half empty are pessimists, and the half full people are optimists. I've used this analogy as a way to illustrate to clients how subtle perceptions can alter their worldview. When they look at the glass, they're actually seeing their own reactions to life.

Now, when Brad's parents looked at Brad, they expected to see a completely full glass. After all, they were prosperous, hard-working people themselves, and they could envision nothing less than a full glass for Brad at all times. Sometime around Brad's early adolescence, however, they began to perceive that Brad's glass was less than full, for he began to operate below their expectations. In their minds, they had worked hard to fill Brad's glass all the way to the brim, and Brad kept behaving and performing in a way that made the contents of that full glass spill out. This produced feelings of frustration, anger, and disappointment in his parents.

The only optimism they had about Brad's future was centered not around what Brad was capable of achieving on his own but rather on what they had provided. He was expected to mirror their success—a success that mirrored their definition. Brad's future was not really about him and actually all about them. Brad had no identity of his own; he was merely a reflection of his parents' desires. Naturally, he was terrified of having to make it on his own as an adult. He had no vision for his own future because he had become convinced he brought nothing to the table of his life.

Somewhere around fifteen years of age, Brad decided he wasn't capable—that his glass without his parents refilling it was actually completely empty. He turned to alcohol to stem the growing fear and anxiety of reaching adulthood. The more he became caught up in alcohol, the more his behavior became erratic and destructive. *Slosh, slosh* went the contents of his glass. His parents kept pouring in resources, advice, and correction. The faster they filled, the more Brad's sloshing behavior drained his glass and his vision of a positive future.

Now, I believe that everyone is responsible for their own behavior, especially as they arrive at adulthood. In fact, the *R* in SOAR is all about responsibility. But as we identified this pattern of behavior between Brad and his parents, what became clear to me was their total lack of belief in a bright future for Brad—as Brad. He certainly didn't have it, and neither did his parents. The only thing all three seemed able to initially agree on was a paralyzing fear of what Brad's future held.

> When Brad's parents looked at his failures, they saw their own.

Because of their own achievements, Brad's parents couldn't see the true horizon line when they looked at Brad. They kept looking inward at themselves and refused to see Brad for who he was. They looked upward into the stratosphere, setting the bar so high Brad was always viewed as substandard. As his struggles with life increased in adolescence, they began to avoid really looking at Brad at all. It was too painful, for they truly loved their son, but when they looked at Brad's failures, they caught a glimpse of their own.

What this family desperately needed was a restored vision of optimism and hope for the future. Brad's parents needed to believe in God's power to help Brad overcome his drinking. Brad needed to trust God's plan for his life and stop fearing the future. They all needed to grasp God's grace and learn to forgive each other. Fortunately, they've been able to heal and reestablish their relationships, but it took years of diverted time and energy to bring their family back on the right track. I applaud your decision to put your energies into your family now!

Living the Blessing

Gary Smalley and John Trent many years ago wrote a wonderful book called *The Blessing*. One of its basic themes is the importance of parents bestowing a blessing—their vision of a bright future—on their children. It is based on the concept of biblical blessings that were passed along from generation to generation, as seen in Scripture. Smalley and Trent believe a time comes in the life of the maturing child when parents have the vital responsibility of confirming their own steadfast belief in a blessed and successful future for that child. It is an affirmation of the type of adult that child has grown or will grow into. When this blessing is withheld or unavailable, maturing children experience a void in their lives that can last long into adulthood. They will, therefore, spend a great deal of time and energy searching after this acceptance and approval, even if their father or mother is deceased. No success is deemed enough without it.

This idea of blessing your children through a positive belief in their future is what the *O* in SOAR is all about. While a formal declaration of blessing is important, living out this belief day in and day out is also important. But, as Brad's story illustrates, sometimes parents aren't able to see a bright future for their children for a variety of reasons.

Setting Your Sights on God

During flight, times will come when you're simply unable to discern the horizon. Conditions will arise that confuse and confound your human vision. That is why it's always a good idea to know how to fly using instruments. Instruments are not compromised by fatigue or deceived by optical illusions, darkness, or storm. If things get turned upside down, instruments can show what's really right-side-up.

> God's vision cuts through our fog and keeps us grounded in hope.

God is like that for us. When our own view shows nothing but the turbulent, stormy weather of childhood rebellion, or the pitch black of desperation over circumstances, or the dulling monotony of static situations, God is able to provide us with his horizon line of hope. His vision cuts through our fog and keeps us grounded in hope.

Let's take a look at Jeremiah 29:11: "'For I know the plans I have for you,' declares the LORD, 'plans to prosper you and not to harm you, plans to give you hope and a future.'" This passage of hope is found in a book full of catastrophe, outlining the fall, capture, and exile of Jerusalem. It wouldn't seem the ideal place to speak of this kind of hope. Yet Jeremiah chose to see the future through God's eyes. This vision allowed him to endure his own imprisonment and the destruction of his beloved country. This vision allowed him to cry out even then, "The steadfast love of the Lord never ceases, his mercies never come to an end; they are new every morning; great is your faithfulness" (Lam. 3:22–23 NRSV).

Every family goes through struggles, and children have natural ups and downs in their demeanor and growth. But if your child stays in a pattern of stagnation or reversal, envisioning a bright future can be hard. However, I want to remind you how powerful God is. If through all of the struggles of Jeremiah, God was still able to provide and promise a future of hope for his people, surely he is able to give you a vision of hope for your family. From this foundation of assurance, you will be able to share with your family this optimism for their future.

Here are a few more Scriptures for you to meditate on as you strengthen yourself to be a positive and optimistic force for good in your family:

"There is a future hope for you, and your hope will not be cut off" (Prov. 24:14). Again, this is a promise to you and your family that no matter where you are right now or what obstacles you have identified to work through, God is with you.

"Be strong and take heart, all you who hope in the LORD" (Ps. 31:24). As the SOAR vision bearer, your role is to exemplify this hope in your own life. Be strong in your knowledge of what is positive for your family and hold fast to your commitment. Take heart when you encounter inevitable difficulties. Always hope in the Lord for success.

"We wait in hope for the LORD; he is our help and our shield" (Ps. 33:20). This is a reminder that the battle for your family's well-being is not being waged alone: God is your help and shield in this endeavor.

"Be joyful in hope, patient in affliction, faithful in prayer" (Rom. 12:12). Sometimes we can hope in the future but still have a pretty lousy attitude about right now. This verse reminds us to be *joyful* in hope and patient through the struggles. And remember to pray!

"May the God of hope fill you with all joy and peace as you trust in him, so that you may overflow with hope by the power of the Holy Spirit" (Rom. 15:13). This is my absolute prayer for you!

Patient Anticipation

I want to take a moment here to explain what I meant at the beginning of the chapter when I talked about the "joined stalks of positive and patient anticipation." We've already talked about the need to be positive in order to remain optimistic in the future. Let's look at this concept of *patient anticipation*.

I don't know about you, but I struggle with patience. I'm fairly good with optimism, but patience is another thing altogether! Because I am optimistic, I can see that bright future ahead, and I want it right now! Waiting for the good thing you know will come can be hard. It's like waiting for Christmas as a child.

> **Understand that some plans take time to mature and flower to completion.**

God is all about patient anticipation. He sent Christ at "just the right time" (Rom. 5:6). God understands that some plans require time to mature and flower to completion. You will need to exhibit your own patient anticipation as you work with your family on the SOAR concepts. Changes will not happen overnight, and you must remain hopeful and patient. Strive, in a forward-looking manner, to continue on the good path on which you've chosen to take your family.

In order for your family members to accept and exhibit their own optimism, they must also learn the art of patient anticipation. This is the quality that allows us to utilize the vital personal characteristic of *delayed gratification*. Why is optimism tied to delayed gratification? Because pessimism leads to instant gratification. If you have no hope in a better tomorrow, you'd better grab what you can today, regardless of the consequences. If you think the glass is half empty, you tend to drink it right now before the contents get any lower! However, if you believe in a hopeful tomorrow, you can more easily give up temporary comfort for lasting benefits. If you believe the glass is half full, then the contents are rising, and you can wait until it rises all the way to the top!

Delayed gratification is a mature response to life. It is based upon experience and an understanding that you can't always have what you want, when you want it, but you can work toward obtaining what you want in the future. Children, with their limited life experience, can have difficulty with this concept (adults certainly can too!). If they want a thing now, they don't understand why they shouldn't have it. It's why they want to eat cookies before dinner. They're hungry now, cookies taste good, so why not? To them it seems a reasonable request.

As parents, we know this isn't a reasonable request. We know that eating sweets before dinner will fill them up with sugar, processed flour, and fats, and they won't be hungry to eat a nutritious dinner. Now, I'm not saying children should never eat cookies; we'll talk a lot more about this when I outline the *R* in SOAR. Children are the best judges of when they are hungry, but not the best judges of what to eat when they are hungry. They have an immature sense of delayed gratification. However, if your child knows the wonderful dinner you're preparing will be ready soon, they'll more easily say no to cookies now and wait for something better. (Your part of this equation, of course, is to provide the "something better." We'll also talk more about this later.)

> # Optimism
> allows for delayed gratification, while pessimism promotes instant gratification.

Delayed gratification is important in more than food choices. You also need to help children understand that things like learning, growing, and achieving take time and effort. This can be frustrating when a child has a learning disability or has trouble grasping an important academic concept. Children can become disheartened and doubt their ability to overcome the obstacle. This is true over a wide spectrum of ability levels. Highly capable children can be sidetracked by a task or concept that eludes them when many others come easily. Children who take longer to grasp a concept or skill can grow frustrated at their pace of mastery. Wherever they are, the ideals of hard work, perseverance, and gradual progress are vital. This is where patient anticipation comes into play. The anticipation is in knowing that given time, the task will be completed, the concept grasped, the skill mastered. It's that old adage that says, "If at first you don't succeed, try, try again." Optimism motivates the second, third—and tenth—try.

Believing in Your Child's Success

As a parent, watching your child struggle at something can be difficult. Seeing him or her fail can be devastating. Optimism allows you, as a parent, to find the positives in struggle and failure. Your child will experience both many times, and you have the job of cultivating an atmosphere where positives can be found in negatives and where negatives are seen as an inevitable part of life. Setbacks can provide invaluable insight into the situation and the person. If setbacks or failures are seen as disasters, your children will lose hope when these invariably occur.

> If setbacks or failures are seen as disasters, your child will lose hope.

You want your children to know and understand how to positively make use of the setbacks and failures in their lives. Your child might benefit if you read with them the autobiography of a famous person. Choose someone in a field your child is interested in. Successful, accomplished people rarely, if ever, have a life of continual stair-step progress. Most actually have a life punctuated by spectacular failures, each of which taught them an important lesson they were able to use to eventually achieve success. Scripture itself is also full of ordinary people making ordinary mistakes yet finding success trusting in an extraordinary God.

You must be your child's and your family's cheerleader. Often you can more easily motivate those members of the family you are closer to and identify with. You may have a harder time connecting with the withdrawn child or the child who is opposite of your personality or temperament. To be able to communicate a vision of a positive future, you must have established lines of communication with all family members. If you do not, you will need to spend time establishing or restoring those communication lines, which are really the lifelines of your relationship.

> **Lines of communication are the lifelines of your family relationships.**

Take a moment to go back to your journal. Write out a blessing for each family member. What positives do you see for their future? Now, how can you strengthen and nurture those positives? Be honest also about any family members with whom you're having difficulty relating. What is the source of the difficulty? Is it a personality trait in that person? In you? What are three positive steps you can take to improve your communication and relationship with that person? Remember, you must not only believe in the positive future of that person; you also need to communicate that belief in a way that is meaningful and accepted.

Next, I'd like you to write down what your definition of "success" would be for each person's life. After that, note what you believe God's definition of success would be for that person. How close are the two? Are there areas where you need to give up your own definition if it interferes with God's? For example, your definition of success may have to do with the acquisition of material wealth. God promises to bless us and give us what we need, but he does not define a person's success—or value or worth, for that matter—by how much money they have. If that were the case, Christ would have come down with material wealth instead of spending his life on earth being supported monetarily by others. Remember that each member of your family has been given to you as a gift from God. Ultimately, they belong to him, and his definition of success is what will give them the greatest degree of personal satisfaction and blessing. You must pray and ask God to help your definition of success and his definition of success to become one.

> Take time to know your child's definition of personal success.

Next, find a quiet moment with each person and ask what his or her definition of success is. For smaller children, you might frame the question as to what sorts of things make them feel happy or really good about themselves. For older children who understand the concept of success, go ahead and ask the question. Communicate your genuine desire to know their definition. This isn't a time to share what *your* definition is. What I'd like you to do is compare the two definitions. In most cases, you will see areas of difference.

You can help your child understand and appreciate success. Depending upon the age of your child, his or her definition of success may seem to be shallow—winning a game or growing older or physical beauty. But within their definition you can find hints of nascent needs and desires. The child who views success as winning a game may have a higher need for acknowledgment and recognition. The child who views success as growing older may be going through an awkward stage of life or view an older sibling as a role model. The child who views physical beauty as success may harbor feelings of inferiority due to a perceived lack of physical attractiveness. Your job is to help your child understand the true meaning, God's meaning, of success; it is also very much to listen to your child tell you what success means to him or her. In this way you can begin the process of integrating your, God's, and your child's definitions together to help your child SOAR.

Father, thank you for giving me hope and a future. Forgive me when I fail to see through your eyes. Help me to view each member of my family through these eyes of hope. Allow me to convey your confidence in a bright future for my children and my family. Protect me when doubt and fear cloud my sight. Keep me focused always on you! May my family see me as a positive example of living out my faith and trust in you each day. I have so much to be thankful for. I have so much to look forward to! Amen.

4

A Is for Active

Jesus said to them, "My Father is always at his work to this very day, and I, too, am working."

John 5:17

I love this verse because it reveals that God and Christ are both active and achieving. That's really what we want for ourselves and for our families. Need some inspiration? Look to God and Christ. Nothing is passive or static about them. They are engaged in this world—working, busy, accomplishing. Genesis says that after each day of creation, God saw what he had made and declared it "good," even "very good" (see Genesis 1). God is a doer. As we are created in God's image, we are created to be doers also. Helping your family to be active and achieving helps them to find and fulfill their purpose in God.

As we begin to look at the specifics of how to increase the activity of your family, please be aware that it will come with a cost. The cost will come in the form of your time and commitment. We've already discussed how you need to take the lead in providing support and encouragement. If you haven't before equated these with *time*, please do so now. You must spend time with your children, with your family, implementing the changes that need to be made. This will require you to look at what you're currently doing and how you're spending your time and to restructure your day so you can support these changes. This chapter is going to help you do that through scenarios and suggestions from me as well as creative options you'll come up with yourself, given your particular situation.

> Be prepared to give your family the gift of your **time**.

Liftoff!

In our flight analogy, being active is the process of moving forward. In order to leave the ground, a plane must expend a great deal of energy. The plane, which has been stationary or moving slowly, must accelerate to what's called *critical velocity*. That's the point at which the speed of the plane causes enough lift under the wings to propel the airplane airborne. When you're in the plane, you can hear the work of the engines. You can feel your body pushed back into your seat. You can see the increasing speed as the scenery begins to whip past the window. The entire plane is straining to leave the ground.

As you begin working with your family to SOAR, don't be surprised if you feel like you're straining to lift off! You probably are—but keep moving forward, gaining momentum, and you'll be off the ground in no time. During this time, remember to be supportive and optimistic about the outcome. If pilots decided becoming airborne was too hard, all of us would remain permanently grounded.

Children Were Made to Be Active

Children by nature are engaged in a great deal of activity. After all, their brains are constantly growing, evaluating, learning. Likewise, internal activity is part of the process of physical maturation. With all of that existing "activity," why would they need anything more? The answer is that kids' activities support and augment their mental and physical growth. Different types of activities are physical activities, mental/intellectual activities, emotional/relational activities, and spiritual activities. A healthy child engages in all four. Let's take a look at each type.

Physical Activity

One area where today's children are lacking is in physical activity. Much of this has to do with the way our culture has changed over the years. When I was growing up, my mother stayed at home in order to raise me and my sister. We played outside in the neighborhood with other children, most of whose mothers were also home. We rode our bikes, often outside the neighborhood and into town. We walked, ran, climbed, and rode scooters and skateboards. We met after school at school yards, backyards, and vacant lots to play ball or hide-and-seek. We had forts and tree houses. We considered it torture to be *inside* on just about any day the weather wasn't horrible.

> Many children today suffer from a lack of physical activity.

That has changed. The majority of mothers of young children work outside the home. Neighborhoods do not automatically become playgrounds when the last bell sounds at school. Children go to day care, after-school programs, or relatives' homes. Older children are latchkey; they may go home but may also be cautioned to stay inside or in the backyard.

Parents no longer feel they can safely let their children walk unattended in neighborhoods and communities. They see news stories of abductions and wonder what they would do if their own child turned up missing or worse. Sadly, "safe" for many parents has come to mean a form of physical inactivity—don't go outdoors, no walking down the street, stay inside, stay *safe*. The parental sphere of comfort has shrunk significantly, and as it has, so has the amount of physical activity.

> **Parents hamper their children's activities out of fear for their children's safety.**

One of the main causes of childhood obesity is the reduction in the amount of physical activity for our children. (The other main cause is the types of food and drink being consumed, which we'll discuss in a later chapter.) Sedentary, inactive children use less energy. All of that excess energy is stored by their bodies in the form of fat. Excess weight makes moving harder, resulting in a decreased motivation to do so. It becomes a vicious cycle.

The great news, however, is that children are uniquely positioned to lose that weight, given the right conditions. Ideally, growing children should not be encouraged to lose weight. Rather, they should be encouraged to maintain their weight and allow their growing bodies to utilize that excess stored energy in the process of physical maturation. In essence, they will "grow into" their weight.

Your Partner, the Pediatrician

Your primary care physician can be a wonderful partner to help you track your child's body weight and growth progress. Many parents take their children to the doctor only when ill. If your child is currently overweight, I suggest you commit to a regular series of wellness visits with his or her pediatrician. Not only will this communicate the importance you place on physical well-being, it will also provide you with motivation in the form of accountability. You'll have another adult to work with you, a health care professional who can provide insights and knowledge on the physical maturation and healthy growth of your child. This will require a commitment on your part of scheduling, time, and money. Talk to your child's doctor and develop a plan and goals. Work together to determine the appropriate level of activity, duration of activity, and healthy weight for your child. The more overweight your child is, the more critical this component is. You don't want to jeopardize his or her health in order to improve it!

> **Work with your child's pediatrician on a wellness plan.**

Because children's bodies are in the process of growing, they have an important need to engage in all types of physical activities that strengthen and stretch their muscles, tendons, and joints. Physical activity also helps ensure they form adequate bone density. Running, jumping, climbing, stretching, playing bodies are healthy bodies. Think of an image of children running and playing. What do their faces look like? They are smiling, happy, giggling faces, flush with health. This is the way God designed our bodies to react to physical activity, especially the young, growing bodies of our children.

Daily Activity

Children need daily physical activity interspersed throughout the day. In school, this is generally in the form of recess. Don't be complacent, however, and think that recess is sufficient. Many times, especially in upper-elementary-age children, recess can become more a social function and less a time for physical activity. Unfortunately, in many elementary schools and middle schools, what used to be called "PE" for physical education is being pressured by academic reforms. Recently, in my area near Puget Sound, a school district informed parents of elementary-age children that recess will now only be scheduled during the lunch hour. The teacher will have sole discretion as to whether or not students are able to utilize regular recess time. The reason put forth is the need for more instructional classroom time in order to bolster poor academic scores on state-mandated tests. Quite naturally, parents and students are not happy with this development!

School PE time is not enough!

In many high schools around the country, PE is considered an "elective." Students are no longer required to have one class period of PE each day. Some are even able to opt out of PE in order to ensure the proper credits in other subjects in order to graduate. At a time of increased societal obesity, curtailing PE just doesn't make sense, but that is what is happening.

Don't assume your child is getting enough physical activity to be healthy just at school. You must plan to provide more for your child. Children should have at least an hour of physical activity each and every day after school and at least two hours a day on the weekends. This activity time should be highly physical and involve cardiovascular exercise, such as biking, running, skateboarding, ice skating, roller skating, or swimming. When I was growing up, the obvious time to engage in such an extended period of play was from after school to dark. When I was younger, I played with neighborhood kids. As I got older, I joined organized sports and clubs. Today one of the most common physical activity options is the afternoon to early evening sports club or team. Generally these teams make use of local school and park playfields. Coaches and parent volunteers are members of the community and are known by other parents. State background checks for volunteers are common. Practices run several afternoons or evenings per week, with games on weekends. While this is a substantial time commitment for any family, the benefits of organized, intense physical play, sportsmanship, and camaraderie are well worth the effort!

Activity for Younger Children

I've spoken up to this point of school-age children. Let's focus for a moment on toddlers and pre-school-age children. Children younger than five also need sustained physical activity. The duration of this activity, however, is shorter. Toddlers generally can handle 15 to 20 minutes at any one time. Pre-school-age children can generally handle up to 30 minutes at a time. The key for younger children is more frequent opportunities, each for a shorter time period. As children age, they develop the physical stamina to increase the frequency, duration, and intensity of their physical play. If you are the primary caregiver for your young child, you will need to ensure that these opportunities for physical play are present every day. In most cases, you'll need to participate with your child, not only to monitor the activity but also to provide support and guidance during it. For those children approaching school age, look for ways to partner with other parents in your area, perhaps through a co-op or play group. If your child is in a day care situation, ascertain what physical play opportunities are provided each day. Change providers if you are not satisfied. Physical play for your child is vital!

> Younger children need shorter play periods frequently during the day.

School-Age Activities

When your child enters school, I urge you to consider enrolling him or her in an after-school club or organization that provides a variety of physical activities. Boys and Girls Clubs, organized after-school programs, the YMCA, community-based recreation programs, or similar groups are all places to start. Having children engaged and active in an organized setting in the after-school hours benefits the entire community. Idle children can be at-risk children due to their own immature and inventive natures.

Older children can certainly benefit from school or community sports teams. Little League, soccer, karate, basketball, football, and dance are all areas where children can engage in supervised, extended physical activity. What is the cost to you? Well, you will have a financial cost and also a commitment in time. You need to arrange for transportation to and from. You need to commit to being supportive during practice times and game times. Again, these teams often require several days a week for practice and usually a weekend game. Is this a large commitment? Yes, but it is also providing your child with a team atmosphere, physical activity, social interaction, and positive goal-setting.

> Sports offer a team atmosphere, physical activity, social interaction, and positive goal-setting.

Talk to your child about preferences regarding what type of activity he or she would like to engage in. Remember that physical activity is the goal, not necessarily always winning or being the best on the team. Allow your child to make choices, but stress that whichever activity is chosen, the commitment is for the length of the season. Fortunately, most teams are for a set period of time—several months—and your child can then try something else. Encourage your child to try a variety of different activities. Young children tend to do best in team settings, while older children may prefer to try individualized sports such as tennis or track.

For those days without a practice or a game, you will need to work with your child to come up with an alternate activity. Older children may take the dog for a long walk or organize a weekly neighborhood play day. For younger children, you may need to structure your time to allow for a late afternoon or early evening at the park or playfield yourself. Your child needs to learn to positively anticipate an extended period of physical activity each day. This will be immensely beneficial now and will also establish a "norm" that will last into adulthood. The government recommends adults spend one hour per day in physical activity. How much easier will this be for your adult children if you have helped prepare the way all through their childhood? A habit of positively anticipating and engaging in physical activity is a lifelong gift you can give to your child. Help your child "get off the ground" now.

Mental/Intellectual Activity

Just as a child's body is growing and maturing, a child's mind is expanding and learning. Think of the amazing amount of information a child gains during the school years, from age five to eighteen! Of course, learning starts in the womb and just keeps going from there. This is also the way God designed us, as we see in Psalm 139. We were meant to expand and use our minds.

> Just as a child's body is growing, so is the mind.

We grow mentally and intellectually through being challenged and stimulated. When a child is first born, we fill his or her world with colors, sights, and sounds. Their brains are working nonstop to process and assimilate all they are learning. As a child heads into school, his or her brain is working overtime to make sense of this world and to organize and order his or her thoughts and reactions.

Casual Learning

Even with all the mental/intellectual activity that takes place in school, children still have room for more. Learning does take place in the structured environment of a class-room, but it also occurs in the ordinary, day-to-day activi-ties within a family. Deuteronomy 11:19 says, speaking of spiritual concepts, to "teach them to your children, talking about them when you sit at home and when you walk along the road, when you lie down and when you get up." Was the Bible indicating that only spiritual ideas can be conveyed in this fashion? No, the message is that teachable moments abound in our everyday lives with our children.

What parent hasn't taken a walk with a young child and found the "walk" interrupted almost too many times to count? That inquiring little mind has an almost endless amount of questions. "Why is the sky blue?" "Why do leaves look different?" "Why do some bugs crawl and some bugs fly?" "Why does the wind blow?" "Why can't you see the wind?" On and on they go. Any time your child has your undivided attention, he or she has an opportunity to ask you a question and learn something.

Know Your Special Child

Again from Psalm 139 we know that each of us is cre-ated by God in a special way. Verse 13 says that God knit each one of us together in our mother's womb. We are not created from a cookie-cutter mold but crafted specially, individually, by God himself. We are different, and each of us learns and processes information in similar and unique ways. The challenge—and delight—of parents is to know their children well enough to be able to tailor their men-tal/intellectual activities to produce the best results. Some children learn through seeing and analyzing information; they are visual learners. Some children learn through hear-ing and analyzing information; they are auditory learners. Some children learn through touch and experimentation; they are kinesthetic or tactile learners. As every parent knows, no child falls into neat little boxes, and your child will probably be dominant in one style but have aspects of the others as well. (As part of your journaling for this chapter later on, you'll answer some questions to help you identify what style most describes your child.)

Quality and Quantity Time

What is the cost associated with mental/intellectual activity? Especially with younger children, the cost is your *time*. Children require time. Several years ago, as more and more women were entering the workforce, a theory was proposed that said how much time you spent with your children didn't matter as long as it was "quality" time. It was called the "quality versus quantity time" argument. Quality time was defined as time with your child that was meaningful, instructive, and connected. The thought was that a parent could have as much or greater influence on their child through the *quality* of time spent and not merely the *quantity*. The working theory was that even though you might only be with your child for a short period of time each day, if you could make that time *quality time*, your child would be the same or even better off than if you were with them for much longer amounts of time during the day. The main difficulty with this theory, of course, is that children cannot be directed to be receptive on cue. It is important to have *quality* time with your children, but that happens within the context of *quantity*. The more time you can spend interacting with your children, the more circumstances will converge to produce that quality time. Younger children, especially, need lots and lots of your time—as much as you can give them. Older children, quite naturally, are involved in other activities and friends. However, they need to know that you are available to them when they need you. Older children have a tendency to

> **Quality** time happens within the context of a **quantity** of time.

push "quality" time by bringing concerns and questions to you. If you're not available or have no time for them, they will seek the answers and affirmations they need somewhere else—and it may not be a place you approve of.

Working around School Work

Once your child is in school, much of their mental/intellectual activity will be centered around their schoolwork. As a parent, you do not have the job of accomplishing your child's schoolwork, but you can participate in and support that schoolwork. Not only will you be aware of how your child is doing in school, you'll know what is being studied and how it is being presented. For Christian parents, this insight is vital, especially for children in a public school system. Being actively engaged in your child's schoolwork will allow you the opportunity to provide biblical insights and perspectives on secularly presented subjects. You'll keep up with how they're learning and what they're learning!

Now, you don't necessarily need to know everything beforehand. As your child progresses in grades, often it's a mental challenge on your part to keep up! Your job is to be involved, observant, and supportive—to convey your belief in the value of an education and the biblical principle found in Colossians 3:17: "And whatever you do, whether in word or deed, do it all in the name of the Lord Jesus, giving thanks to God the Father through him." *Whatever you do* includes schoolwork, even that difficult math assignment or long English paper.

> Institute a family game night and play the games your child enjoys.

With the intense nature of learning due to schoolwork, other opportunities for mental/intellectual activity with your children can be obscured. I encourage you to find ways to have fun with your children. Institute a family game night—and play the games your child enjoys. If you have several children, rotate the job of designated "gamer" who decides which game is played. Pre-select a variety of games, from board games to card games, for each "gamer" to choose from so no one will choose a surprise game that one child knows but the other child doesn't. Fully participate in these games and use this as an opportunity to relax and enjoy your child within the context of an intellectually engaging or mentally stimulating game. You may be surprised at how often even small children can triumph within a game night setting.

Emotional/Relational Activity

Children, as human beings, are born with emotional range and depth. What parent hasn't been thrilled by their child's first smile or laugh? What parent hasn't been touched by their child's first cry of separation? Children are born with a basic palate of emotional colors; as we get older, we come to appreciate the different hues within those colors. *Happy* as a child becomes content, blissful, ecstatic, and pleased as we grow and mature. *Unhappy* as a child becomes disappointed, frustrated, lonely, and rejected also as we grow up. Do we have all of these emotions as babies? Yes, I believe we do, but as we mature we're able to identify them and place them into context. A ten-year-old should be able to respond to disappointment over not getting a wanted item at the store differently than a two-year-old. The disappointment may be similar, but the response should be different because of experience and growth. Just as our bodies and thoughts mature, so does our emotional makeup.

Emotional Relationships

Emotions in children tend to focus around relationships: relationship with self, others, and the world. Each child has a relationship with him- or herself. Some need constant outside stimulation, while others are content to engage in self-directed play. As children, we develop the habit of "self-talk"—those internal messages that help us cope with who we are, what happens to us, and how we feel about it. Some children have positive self-talk; they are able to look at circumstances with an upbeat point of view. They believe in themselves and are naturally optimistic. Other children have negative self-talk; they are innately uncertain, fearful, or disparaging. Their internal dialogue does not support them; rather, it undermines them. You need to know the tenor of your child's self-talk. You can often determine this by observing your child engaged in a self-directed task. Is he calm and focused? Does she become frustrated at a setback? Is he excited about an accomplishment? Does she come to share her victories with you or a sibling? Is he able to stay on task until it is completed? Does she sing or talk to herself while engaged? Watch how your child reacts to himself when he thinks no one else is watching. Be aware of any verbalization she makes while playing.

Watch for the tenor of your child's self-talk.

Children also develop emotional relationships with others. They learn who their mother and father, brother and sister, and grandparents are. They are aware of *other* and what that means. Children can react in neutral, positive, or negative ways to the presence of others in their lives. They start out with a small circle of relationships, which expands as they grow older. Healthy children are those who are able to enjoy and appreciate a diversity of relationships. They appreciate who they are and allow for relationships to develop with those outside themselves and their families.

Your child may appear shy or socially isolated. Recognize that what you interpret as shyness may simply be a predilection for different activities than you participated in growing up. You may be a gregarious, outgoing type of person who loves engaging in new social situations. Your child may have a more introverted personality. This isn't to say he or she can't enjoy the occasional crowd; he or she simply may need more time to adjust. Just because your child doesn't react as you do doesn't mean something is wrong.

> **If your child reacts differently in social situations than you, this doesn't mean something is wrong.**

If your child is shy or socially isolated, he or she will need more support to extend outward. It won't be natural, and it shouldn't be forced. Rather, your job will be to understand what is behind this isolation and work to foster more interaction with others. Observe what circumstances are the least threatening to your shy child. It may be inviting a single friend over to play, as opposed to the entire neighborhood. It may include a trip to the library or "quiet" space, as opposed to always choosing a play environment. Work with your child to prepare him or her for stressful situations. Seek to ascertain the basis for his or her trepidation or fear. Often, these reasons will point you directly to the pattern of negative self-talk that undermines his or her ability to trust in spontaneous situations. If this pattern is pervasive and resistant to change, I encourage you to seek out a Christian counselor for your child. This childhood self-talk is carried throughout adulthood, and you want it filled with hope and optimism from God's point of view. A child mental health specialist can work with you and your child to "rewrite" those messages and allow your child to relax and enjoy who he or she is, regardless of the situation.

The Damage of Social Isolation

As you think about what activities would benefit your child, don't forget to consider the emotional/relational component. One unfortunate aspect of our current culture is an increasing amount of social isolation. Many children leave school and go home to an empty house for several hours. Some go home and immediately engage in activities on a computer or an electronic game that involve no other person. Families tend to live apart from extended family. Neighbors don't know neighbors or their children. Teachers are overworked and overbooked, with little time for individual students.

> **Children need to interact with and appreciate many different types of people.**

Busy, harried parents prefer to keep to themselves and fail to join social clubs, religious organizations, or community groups that might allow for their children to interact with other children and adults. Kids' school friends are just that—friends at school only, as working parents make playing together after school a sporadic activity at best.

Simply put, children need to be around other people, and not just family. Family is a great place to start, especially extended family, but it shouldn't stop there. Children need to learn how to interact with and appreciate many different types of people. This is hampered by the recent rise in concern among parents about leaving their children in the care of other adults, be they parents of a friend, scout leaders, coaches, day care workers, or in some cases even family. The continuous news cycle has been both a positive and a negative. It has alerted parents to the potential for abuse in seemingly "normal" situations, but it has also, by its emotional impact, frightened parents. You don't want your children hurt, but herding them into a sheltered "bubble" of just your family can be damaging also.

Become Involved Yourself

One of the best ways to juggle both your child's need for social interaction and your concern for his or her safety is to become engaged yourself in the activity or event. Get to know the adults and other children involved. Volunteer for the organization or event. Be around. Be available. Don't just get your child there and leave as soon as possible. Observe your child. Know what happens so you can help your child process his or her experiences when the activity is completed.

What's the cost? Besides the financial cost of an organized group, one of the costs is, again, your time. Another cost is involvement. You must be involved and observant, even if you are not the primary leader of the group.

Don't just drop your child off— **participate!**

In our busy, fast-paced world, we can be strongly tempted to use these extracurricular activities as a "break." While this can certainly be okay every once in a while, I caution against habitually just dropping them at the field. Children feel important when you make them important. Just being on the sidelines or in the bleachers to watch your child communicates their value. Besides, you'll be personally present to watch the large and small victories! They'll be more meaningful to your children if you can share the experience instead of being told about it by a stranger.

As your child learns more about the activity, game, or sport, you can learn more about your child. Be alert to how your child reacts to others. How do other adults react to your child? How do the other children? How does your child react to situations and circumstances? Are those reactions mostly positive or negative? Is your child outgoing and confident with others? Is he fearful and shy? Is she rude or disrespectful? This will help you be aware of how your child is doing emotionally and relationally.

Spiritual Activity

One of the most bonding activities you can do with your child is to jointly express your spiritual nature before God.

In this area, especially, children can often end up the teacher. Jesus said in Matthew 19:14 that the kingdom of God belongs to children. Within their innocent questions and uncomplicated conclusions, children are able to grasp deep spiritual concepts. Our adult minds go off into all sorts of theological tangents, sometimes causing us to become spiritually knotted up. A casual comment or earnest question by a child has a way of untangling our arguments and pointing the way back to the truth.

As you look for healthy activities for your child, don't forget the spiritual. Spend time each day in prayer with your child. Many parents find bedtime for their children to be a wonderful time for spiritual bonding. My wife, LaFon, and I read to our young sons from the Bible each night and pray together with them. We also incorporate spiritual concepts and ideas into our everyday activities and conversations. We make God a regular, normal, integrated part of our family life. What is the cost of this? You must remain genuine at all times with your children. Your demeanor must be consistent—no "church" personality and "home" personality. In order to instruct your children about God and model Christ to them, you must accept that how you live your life is an open book for your children to read and interpret.

> Make God a regular, normal part of your family life.

I am amazed how many parents spend volumes of time and energy making sure Johnny does his homework and Susie gets to her soccer practice but put almost no time or thought into preparing their children spiritually. They will get their children to church on Sunday and drop them off at Sunday school, assuming their job of spiritual instruction has been completed. They may be at weekday sports practices and every Saturday game—rooting, cheering, being involved—but adopt a completely passive posture when it comes to spiritual issues with their children. If you find yourself falling into this trap, listen to the words of the apostle Paul in 1 Timothy 4:8: "For physical training is of some value, but godliness has value for all things, holding promise for both the present life and the life to come."

While the other types of activities discussed in this chapter are certainly important, don't shortchange your children for the present life and the life to come by neglecting to create, support, and maintain meaningful spiritual activities. I've put down a few suggestions for you. Feel free to adopt these or come up with your own.

1. Take him to church.
2. Make sure she gets to Sunday school.
3. Plan for him to go to summer Bible camp.
4. Allow her to be involved in a midweek church group.
5. Pray and read the Bible together daily.
6. Allow time for your child to ask questions about what you've read together.
7. Talk about spiritual concepts as a part of everyday life.
8. Be open and transparent to your children about your own faith.
9. Share your personal testimony with your children.
10. Praise God for your children in their presence.
11. Act as if they truly are the gift of God they represent, even when they don't act like it!
12. Place your children firmly on the altar of the Lord by praying for them.
13. Read spiritual resources that will help you teach and model your faith in God and Christ.

> **The spiritual time you spend with your child will enrich every other activity.**

The spiritual activity you engage in with your child will enrich and flavor every other activity, whether physical, mental/intellectual, or emotional/relational. Just as Christ "holds all things together" (Col. 1:17), your spiritual activity bonds your family and all your other activities together. Don't neglect this vital part of your family and your child's life!

Real World Solutions

Now, all of this probably sounds just great—in theory—but how do you pull it off in the "real world"? Let's take a look at a typical time-crunched parent, using a father in a two-income household as an example. He gets up early (earlier, in fact, than he'd really like, given when he got to bed the night before) to get ready for work and help get the kids ready to go off to day care or school. With moments to spare, he's dropping off kids at the bus stop or day care. All day is taken up with work, and before he knows it, it's time to go home. If he gets off work earlier than his wife, he's probably the one who picks up the kids. If not, they're already home by the time he arrives. Dinner is eaten, homework is done, and all he wants is just a little bit of time to himself to unwind. In fact, he looks forward to when the kids are finally in bed so he's able to spend some time with his wife.

When life is like this, finding ways to become *more involved* and spend *more time* with your children is hard. Hard, but not impossible. Here are a few suggestions I have for this dad:

- Get up early enough to sit down and have breakfast with your children.
- Take time the night before to choose a particular verse of Scripture to share with them as you eat together.

- Use the time you have in the car with them to reaffirm your love and your desire for them to have a good day and to pray with them.
- After work, take part in an organized activity with your children.
- Take your children to the library on another day of the week.
- Participate together in a midweek church service or Bible study.
- Walk the family dog to a local park together.

In other words, get out of the house and commit time to what makes your children happy. Sure, the easy thing to do is to come home each evening and determine, based upon your day, that the best thing to do is sit on the couch or in front of the television or computer doing just what you want to do. But your children need you to reserve time and energy and involvement for them, especially the younger the child. What is the cost? It means you won't be able to watch that television show or get on the computer as much. It means you'll need to reorient your focus from what you want to do in the evening to what's best for your children. I think you'll find, however, that the rewards of this connected, involved, and active time with your children will far outweigh the costs.

> Reserve some of your time and energy **each day** for your children.

Remember also that having your children with you in the evening is not necessarily the same as being with your children. Having them accompany you to various activities in the evening is fine, but this is not the kind of one-on-one, personal time children need to feel connected. If your children are just along for the ride, this doesn't really constitute time with your children. Evaluate your commitments and make adjustments to allow evenings during the week when your children have your undivided attention.

Take a look at the above suggestions, then look at your situation and be creative. I know of one set of parents who worked forty-five minutes from home. Because of housing prices, they lived in an outlying suburb and commuted into the city for work. They chose to place their young daughter in a day care setting near their work rather than near their house. In this way the forty-five-minute drive to work was done with their daughter. It was time to talk, listen to music, and pray together. The parent who wasn't driving could even sit in the backseat and read a book with their daughter on occasion. Each weekday, this family had ninety minutes of family time in the car. When she became school-age, they were able to sell their home and move closer to work, even though it meant sacrificing a larger house for one closer to the city so their commute time was reduced. Their daughter has recently left home for college. Believe me when I say they've never regretted making decisions with time for their daughter in mind, especially now that they see the results!

> A difficult situation is an **opportunity** for creativity.

Activity Overload

Although it is obviously important for your child to be active, I want to voice a caution here. I see far too many children—and families—who are on activity overload. Their time is so structured and measured out that no time is left for spontaneity or relaxation. Instead of the activity adding to the life of the child or family, activity takes over. Activities are important, but so is rest and rejuvenating— "down time"—especially at home with the family.

Ecclesiastes says "to every thing there is a season, and a time for every purpose under the heaven" (Eccles. 3:1

KJV). During each day, there is certainly a time for your children to be active. But as the hours wind down to evening, your children need to enter a time of restful calm so they are prepared to sleep and "turn off" those active minds and bodies. Every person, especially a growing child, needs a restful, renewing night's sleep. Your child will need this type of sleep in order to have the energy to operate in a healthy range of activities during the day.

> **For your child to take advantage of the day, he or she needs a good night's rest.**

The Need for Rest

Truly restful sleep must be planned for. Several years ago I worked with the frustrated parents of a grade school child who absolutely refused to go to bed easily. Every night was a battle. While additional issues needed to be addressed, one of the primary things we looked at was the mood in the home at bedtime. This young couple worked outside the home, arriving home at around 6:00 p.m. after fighting traffic to get to their child's day care center. Each night of the week, they had some activity, either for the child or for the parents. Dinner was usually rushed or in the car on the way. After these activities, they still had to deal with schoolwork, chores, and baths. Right up until the moment of lights out, the family was operating full speed ahead. Simply put, their child was continually overstimulated by sights, sounds, hustle, and bustle. The rest of the day was a headlong rush that smacked right into "bedtime," whether she was ready or not. Most evenings, she was not.

I suggested this family evaluate the level of activities and intentionally plan a transition time between the high energy of daytime activities and the abrupt cessation in the evening. The first step I encouraged was turning off the television in the house for at least an hour before bedtime. Likewise any loud radio, CD, or computer, although quiet music was perfectly appropriate. They reduced the light level in the house using subdued lighting and candles. Next, I suggested this child take her bath closer to bedtime, during this time of quiet. And what this child really needed was some quiet, connected time with mom and dad— to snuggle in her pajamas and a blanket and be read to or listened to, to sing a song, or just to talk about her day. What she needed was closure. Without it, sleep seemed like a "tearing away" from the frenetic pace. After she went to bed, the television often just stayed off. Lights stayed low. Voices stayed low. Not only was this child able to enjoy more restful sleep, so were her parents!

> **Children need time to transition from activity to rest.**

I cannot emphasize enough the all-around benefits of restful sleep. Children need eight to nine hours of sleep each night. Some children will need more—especially when going through a growth spurt, dealing with a particularly challenging time in school or sports, or fighting off a cold or infection. Some children are so high-energy and high-metabolism that they tend to "hit the wall" and need plenty of sleep to replenish.

Overactive often means under-rested. The day has only so many hours, and adults tend to trade sleep for activity. Inadvertently, this attitude and practice can seep into the scheduling and sleep patterns of their children as well. God designed the day and the night. We need to honor that design in our families by respecting a day full of beneficial activities and planning for a night full of replenishing rest.

Father, you are the Creator of day and night, each unique and beneficial. Help me to evaluate the activities of my family and make positive changes. I want my children to know the blessing of physical health, stamina, and an active life. I also want them to experience the refreshment you give through rest and sleep. Grant me wisdom to evaluate my family's day and night activities and bring them more in line with healthy boundaries. Amen.

5

A Is for Achievement

Jesus said to them, "My Father is always at his work to this very day, and I, too, am working."

John 5:17

Yes, this verse again! Why? Because activity and achievement are interrelated, or at least they should be. Something can be said for activity for activity's sake, but we need to be involved in activities that produce positive results. Without those results, our motivation and enthusiasm for the activity wanes and we quit. As we remember from the last chapter, God is both active and achieving. He is working and producing results in our lives.

A Sense of Accomplishment

Children need to be involved in activity, but they also need to gain from those activities. Yes, children need time for simple, unadulterated play. They also need activities designed to give them a sense of accomplishment and help them discover their gifts and talents from God. Let's take a look at the first aspect.

Achievements don't come from only what you're good at.

One of the most natural ways for children to feel a sense of accomplishment is to learn to do their best at *all* the tasks they are asked to do. It is far too easy to look for achievement only in the things you are good at. Often these don't seem like accomplishments because they come easily. However, when we are able to pull off the difficult or challenging, we recognize we've really accomplished something. Maturity happens when we accept these tasks, whether or not we particularly like them, and strive to do our best. We must learn to take intrinsic (or inner) pride in our achievements, as opposed to always looking for extrinsic (or outside) rewards. We want to feel good about ourselves, within ourselves, and not wait merely for the approval of others.

Academic Achievement

Our ability to achieve today helps us have confidence in tomorrow. Children know and understand they are expected to achieve in life, whether this expectation is expressly voiced or not. In our culture, children are asked to participate and do their best in academic pursuits. School and homework comprise a significant portion of a child's day during three-fourths of the year. How well the child does in school concerns parents, teachers, school administrators, and the child.

For a child to achieve academically does not mean that the child must excel academically. Rather, children achieve academically when they live up to their potential, whatever level that is. Children have different skills, aptitudes, and intellectual capacity. Within that God-designed framework is an achievement level for your child. Your job as a parent is to know where that level is, through active observation and consultation with your child's educators, and to support your child in reaching his or her academic goals.

Your child's teacher can be an asset or a hindrance to these goals. Most teachers are enthusiastic, optimistic professionals who advocate for their students. Occasionally you will find a teacher who simply does not mesh with your child. The only way for you to find out is to be active and involved in your child's school and schoolwork. You are your child's academic coach, even if you engage other professional services to assist your child, like tutoring or special classes. You cannot rely on others to advocate for your child; you must accept this role with enthusiasm, grace, and perseverance.

> **You** are your child's academic coach.

Why this emphasis on academic achievement? How well a child does in school establishes, in many ways, the level of success he or she will have as an adult. Within an academic environment, basic skills are learned and mastered. Without these basic skills—reading, writing, communication, logical reasoning, and mathematic understanding—a child's ability to obtain gainful employment as an adult is severely compromised. Simply put, we live in an academically dependent, technological society.

Because of this emphasis on school, your child is aware that he or she is expected to do well. Most children want to do well in school and are excited to learn, to explore, to discover, and to grow. Your job is to structure your family time to honor and support academic pursuits. Take an interest in school and be aware of what your child is learning. Volunteer in the classroom whenever you are able. Keep in contact with your child's teacher and work together to maximize your child's potential.

God's Gift for Your Child

Life, however, is not completely about school—even for school age children. God has specific things in mind for your child. In order to accomplish his purposes, he has blessed your child with gifts and talents. One area of achievement for your child will be to begin the process of discovering what those gifts and talents are. Often the only way to do that is to try a wide variety of activities. As your child tries things, be alert to ways he or she consistently "shines." Often it may be in unexpected ways. For example, your child may be the sort who enjoys testing out new things. His gift may be a courageous, buoyant spirit that will allow him to serve the Lord as an adult in bold ways. Her gift may be in empathizing with children on the fringe, foreshadowing a gift of concern for the lost. His gift may be a compliant, supportive spirit that helps him contribute to the accomplishments of others.

> Help your child discover his or her God-given gifts and talents.

Look for achievement in more than just accomplishing a task. Often the key to what God has in mind is not in the task itself but in how the task is accomplished and what it says about the person in the process. Even if your child doesn't turn out to be ultimately successful at the activity, you can help them understand and appreciate what they've learned about themselves along the way. *Achievement*, in God's sight, is not limited to the world's idea of *success*. As you are helping your child achieve, remember to be alert to what God considers to be positive characteristics—faithfulness, perseverance, a cheerful spirit, patience, kindness—as well as accomplishment.

Knowing How Your Child Learns

Each child has a way of learning which resonates with them. I spoke earlier about visual, auditory, and tactile (or kinesthetic) learners. What type is your child? Understanding how your child processes information (and even how you do too) will help you tailor instruction to a form that is most readily integrated. Now, I realize that not every lesson can be tailored to a specific learning style, but as a parent, you can come to know your child well enough to target those methods that will produce the best results.

Visual Learner

Is your child a visual learner?

- Does he need to see a whole broken into pieces to understand fractions?
- Does drawing the parameters of a math word problem help her find an answer?
- Does he draw or doodle as a way to relax?
- Does she need to see someone else swing a baseball bat in order to learn the correct stance and swing?
- Does he appreciate pictures of people and places he is learning about?
- Does she take a lot of notes when studying?
- Does he like you to write down his chores?

Consider the ways you've developed to communicate information to your child. I know one mother who always made sure her daughter was looking her directly in the eyes—in other words, that she had her child's attention—before giving instructions. In order for her daughter to internalize the instructions, she needed to see her mother's face and expressions. She was a visual learner.

Auditory Learner

Is your child an auditory learner?

- Can he find what he's looking for just by following your verbal instructions?
- Does she sing or talk to herself when studying or playing?
- Does he watch a person who is talking and remember what was said?
- Are her friends those children who like to talk a lot and are verbally responsive?
- Does he repeat your instructions over and over to himself in order to remember them?
- After meeting new people, does she remember what they were wearing or aspects of their appearance?
- Would he rather listen to a tape or CD than read a book?

Auditory learners make a connection to what is said and who is saying it. Anything that gets in the way of them connecting with the speaker is distracting. Visual learners like to watch from a distance to gauge a situation, while auditory learners tend to jump right into the middle of things and engage in conversation.

Kinesthetic Learner

Is your child a kinesthetic learner?

- Do written or verbal instructions make him fidget?
- Would she rather just start working on a project and learn as she goes?
- Is it hard for him to sit still for long stretches of time?
- When given a choice, would she rather go outside and play than stay inside and read?

- Is his room messy, although he knows where everything is?
- Does she tend to remember how people were feeling after speaking to them, as opposed to what they said or how they were dressed?
- Does he use his hands to gesture when talking or explaining?

Tactile or kinesthetic kids are the kind who need to just jump in and learn. As such, it's best to be available to them when teaching a new skill or explaining a task. They are often very quick to catch on, but only after they've experienced it firsthand.

Again, most people exhibit traits in all categories, so as you're watching your child, simply look for dominance in one area. Then tailor your interactions to ways that easily connect with your child. You'll also be alert to those skills and activities that may come naturally to your child and those that may present challenges. For example, when choosing books for your children to read, visual learners will enjoy bright, bold pictures with lots of people, place, and thing descriptions. Auditory learners will connect best with books that detail conversations and dialogues, such as plays. Kinesthetic learners latch on to emotions and feelings, along with heightened drama.

Accept your child for the unique individual he or she is. Accept yourself for the way you were made. These different styles are not in competition with each other, and one is not "better" than another. God created each of us differently—for a reason.

God's Wisdom

God has designed each of us differently, but we have similarities. No matter what your child's style, God created him or her to be active and achieving. He created us to have an effect upon this earth and the people around us.

In Scripture, the opposite of being active and achieving is to be lazy. Often God demonstrates positive characteristics by emphasizing the negatives of their opposites. The book of Proverbs, especially, contains numerous warnings against developing a habit of underachieving (called laziness) and inactivity (called being a sluggard). Since God devotes quite a bit of his Word to this topic, let's take a look at what he has to say that can help your family SOAR:

> If a man is lazy, the rafters sag; if his hands are idle, the house leaks.
>
> Ecclesiastes 10:18

Within this verse is a vital lesson for each child: the concept of personal responsibility. If you don't take care of your own business, it probably won't get done. We'll talk about responsibility in the next chapter, but I want you to understand how this affects your child. If he develops a pattern of underachieving, he will always be dependent upon others to help provide those things he should be able to provide for himself. God wants us to become equipped to be able to give to others. The lazy person not only needs others to care for her, she is not able to care for others.

> Lazy hands make a man poor, but diligent hands bring wealth.
>
> Proverbs 10:4

Developing a habit of underachieving, or operating below potential, does not bode well for your child's ability to make a living as an adult. God gives us a warning and a promise in this passage. The warning is that being lazy won't help your financial situation. The promise is that hard work produces positive results. Notice that God doesn't say anything about the intelligent or the fortunate or the skilled; he gives this promise to the diligent, something every child can learn to be. Your child will bless you later in life when you've helped her internalize a positive work ethic that doesn't shirk from hard work but perseveres.

> The plans of the diligent lead to profit as surely as haste leads to poverty.
>
> Proverbs 21:5

One of the characteristics of the diligent is that they make *plans*. One way you can assist your child in achieving his potential is the concept of organization. This involves setting goals and coming up with incremental, achievable steps to complete that goal. Help your child by modeling and teaching personal organization such as goal setting and time management.

> Whatever your hand finds to do, do it with all your might.
>
> Ecclesiastes 9:10

Diligence and hard work are habits that apply to any endeavor. At the end of the day, knowing you've done a good job—at school, at play, at activities, at work—carries its own reward. Children who zestfully engage in life see results, which bring a hopeful and positive anticipation for similar results in the future.

> How long will you lie there, you sluggard? When will you get up from your sleep?
>
> Proverbs 6:9

Sometimes I think this verse is speaking specifically about teenagers on the weekends! At least it does illustrate how inactivity breeds inactivity. When a person is not busy and active, they don't have much to look forward to. Even necessary tasks are left undone. Lack of activity slowly saps the strength of will and of body. The inertia caused is extremely difficult to overcome. For your child's sake, help her to avoid this trap.

> A sluggard does not plow in season; so at harvest time he looks but finds nothing.
>
> Proverbs 20:4

This verse brings up an interesting point—it doesn't talk about a lack of plowing but plowing that is not "in season." Activity for activity's sake, again, does not always produce the desired results. Half-hearted, ill-timed efforts will not lead to achievement. Help your children to be wise in when and how they act, looking ahead to the future. This will help anchor the valuable concept of delayed gratification we spoke of earlier. When they plow at the right time, "in season," they will see results.

Making Plans of Your Own

You've seen how important positive activity and achievement are to your child. Now I'd like you to journal specifically how you will help each child be an active and achieving member of the family. (This is very appropriate to do or at least share with the other parent or other significant caregivers to each child.) Spend significant time on this exercise of evaluating what's happening right now—hours, in fact. Consider, meditate, and pray about it. You're going to create a snapshot of what's happening right now in your child's life and what effect this is having on your child.

Look at the grid below. You can use something like this to evaluate the current activities of your children. After the grid, you'll see a detailed explanation and a couple of scenarios using the grid.

Name, Age of Child: _____

Major Activity (such as school, day care, church, sports, extracurricular activities, friends, or whatever your child spends significant time doing): _____

	Positives about activity	Negatives about activity
Physical impacts		
Mental/intellectual impacts		
Emotional/relational impacts		
Spiritual impacts		

Greatest positives for this activity: _____
_____
_____

Greatest negatives for this activity: _____
_____
_____

Possible changes to be made to this activity: _____
_____
_____

For each child, use a separate grid for each major activity your child is currently engaged in. Include school, groups, sports—everything you know your child is involved in. If you have trouble remembering all of the activities, start a list with Monday's activities and go through the week, then construct a grid for each activity.

In the middle column, I want you to list all the positives this activity brings to your child. You'll see that these benefits are separated into the four areas we've talked about—physical, mental/intellectual, emotional/relational, and spiritual. In the last column, I want you to list the negatives. These can be negatives to that child specifically or to the family in general. Be honest about the negatives. You can't change a situation unless you're willing to accept the valid reasons for change.

Here are a few scenarios to help you understand how this grid may help you:

Name, Age of Child: Patrick, 10
Major Activity: Computer video games

	Positives about activity	**Negatives about activity**
Physical impacts	Hand-eye coordination skills	Sedentary—just sits around for hours playing
Mental/intellectual impacts	Has to think quickly to play the game	Wants to play games instead of doing homework
Emotional/relational impacts	Can get out frustrations by "vegging out" in front of game	Game played by himself; doesn't want to interact with the rest of the family
Spiritual impacts	Appreciation to God for sheer "fun" of playing the games	Some games have high degree of violence; might cause desensitization to the pain of others

Greatest positives for this activity: Allows Patrick some "down time" after school, and he really likes playing them.
Greatest negatives for this activity: Games very compelling—he wants to play by himself more than interact with the family.
Possible changes to be made to this activity: Monitor amount of time being played and use as a motivation to complete other tasks.

Name, Age of Child: Angela, 13
Major Activity: Talking to friends on the phone

	Positives about activity	**Negatives about activity**
Physical impacts	With cell phone, can walk around and do things while talking	Just as easy to sit or lay around and talk
Mental/intellectual impacts	Might be discussing or brainstorming school projects	Might just be spending time talking about "nothing"
Emotional/relational impacts	Able to stay connected with other people, including parents if needed	Provides opportunity for gossip or negative talk about others
Spiritual impacts	Can be used to call and speak with other kids from church who don't live nearby	Conversations could become inappropriate

Greatest positives for this activity: Allows Angela to stay connected to other people.
Greatest negatives for this activity: Could be abused by talking too much, connecting with inappropriate people, or discussing inappropriate topics.
Possible changes to be made to this activity: Consider utilizing a plan with a set number of minutes in order to set limits. Monitor cell phone records to note what numbers are being called regularly.

Name, Age of Child: Dominick, 6
Major Activity: Day care

	Positives about activity	**Negatives about activity**
Physical impacts	Able to engage in physical play during the day in supervised setting	Small playground area, not always able to really run and stretch; not able to play outdoors in bad weather
Mental/intellectual impacts	Crafts and activities after school	Sometimes crafts and activities are not intellectually challenging; spends so much time at day care, little time in evening for reviewing school activities
Emotional/relational impacts	Able to interact with other children and adults	Spends hours apart from family members; may think parents put more value in work than in him
Spiritual impacts	Biblical teaching possible if Christian-based day care	If not Christian environment, could be learning and being influenced by secular ideas and priorities

Greatest positives for this activity: Allows for parent(s) to work and bring in an income.
Greatest negatives for this activity: Dominick doesn't want to spend so much time away from family and home.
Possible changes to be made to this activity: Consider the financial implications of reducing time at work, going to a partial schedule, in order to reduce the amount of time Dominick is at day care.

These scenarios are meant as illustrations. If you come up with a method that seems to work better for you—go ahead! The object of this exercise is not to fill out the grid "correctly" but to honestly evaluate each child and his or her activities to determine what is working and what isn't.

Be aware of areas where the positive activity of one child may inadvertently create a negative for another child. Also note areas where your own activities or those of your spouse positively or negatively impact areas of your child's life. Remember, you are doing this exercise with the entire family in mind.

Next, highlight the areas of greatest negative impact for each child. List these separately on a new page. Your job will be to decide what changes you and your family can make to mitigate the negatives. Think "outside the box" for answers. Cast vision for what solutions would truly be the most effective, even if you cannot currently see a way for them to happen. Remember, God is actively involved in your family and wants the very best for you. Jesus specifically said, "with God all things are possible" (Matt. 19:26). So don't leave something out just because you think it's unlikely. The more unlikely it is, the more ripe it is for prayer!

Take Time to Reevaluate

If you're doing this in the summer—or non-school time—you'll want to be sure to do it again for the fall. If you're doing this during school, be just as detailed about activities during the summer months. If your child is not yet in school, you'll surely want to modify this plan when school begins. Use this grid to help assess the positives and negatives of any new activity. In fact, every six months you should review your SOAR plan and make necessary modifications. You might use your child's birthday and a significant holiday in the other half of the year to remind you it's time to review.

Accepting the Cost of Change

This isn't meant to be an easy, quick exercise. You're looking at ways to change fundamental patterns of your family for good. For example, you may determine, like the commuting couple with a young daughter I mentioned before, that where you live in relation to where you work is simply *not* working. Would you be willing to move? If the amount or span of hours required by your job is not working for your family, would you be willing to get another job? If your children simply need more of your time and effort, would you consider giving up work, community, or other involvements to be more available for your children? Ultimately, helping your family to SOAR is going to require sacrifice on your part. What are those sacrifices? What changes do you see need to be made in order to promote the health of your family?

To help motivate you to face and implement these sacrifices, I'd like you to take some time now to think about and record in your journal the positive goals you believe can be accomplished by these sacrifices—in other words, what are *you* achieving? Look at each child individually and then the family as a whole. How will each member of the family be built up by these changes? In turn, how will the family benefit by the building up of each member?

> Focusing on the positive of goals can help you see past the negative of sacrifice.

Now, not every positive change can or should be instituted overnight. If some can offer an immediate benefit and are feasible, why not make the change now? For others, you will need to take some time to think about the implications and plan how to best implement the change. Items like moving or altering an employment situation are quite complicated. Items like cutting down on your son's computer time can be done fairly easily—though explaining why may be much harder!

Spend time this week praying about positive changes for your family. Ask for God's wisdom and confirmation of what you've uncovered so far. Ask him to continue the process of revelation as you look over what you've done. Ask for strength and courage to talk about these changes with the other adults who impact your family. Ask for peace of mind and heart as you become convinced of what you must do to be a positive force in your family and help each member to SOAR.

Father, I know you want me to make my family the priority of my life. Sometimes, I confess, I struggle knowing how. Grant me wisdom to see where I need to make changes. When I look at my children, at my family, I so want each one to be happy, active, and achieving the potential you gave them. Help me to trust you enough to wait for your answers with faith that those answers will come. Give me the courage to do what is needed in response to your answers. As I model an active and achieving life myself, be with me and give me strength. Amen.

6

R Is for Responsible for My Body

> Therefore, I urge you, brothers, in view of God's mercy, to offer your bodies as living sacrifices, holy and pleasing to God—this is your spiritual act of worship. Do not conform any longer to the pattern of this world, but be transformed by the renewing of your mind. Then you will be able to test and approve what God's will is—his good, pleasing and perfect will.
>
> Romans 12:1–2

Scripture tells us that we are responsible to offer our bodies to God as a living sacrifice. We need to view our bodies as a valuable resource for God's purposes in the world. In addition, we are to align our thoughts, priorities, and values not according to the pattern of this world but according to God's will. These are lofty goals. We need to model them as adults so we can teach them to our children. We must show our children—not merely tell our children—how to act as responsible citizens in God's kingdom.

Now, it's hard enough for adults to act responsibly! To give our children ample opportunities to integrate personal responsibility into their code for living, we must start early and teach often. That's where you come in. Through the *R* in SOAR, you're teaching your children to think of themselves as belonging to God. Not only will this result in God's blessing in their lives, it will give them a sense of belonging, connection, and lifelong purpose. These lessons are invaluable in helping your child understand that an entire world of possibilities and motivations exists outside of him- or herself. This allows your child to have a service-oriented, outward focus, as opposed to a self-centered, inward focus. And this shift in focus is at the heart of maturation as an adult.

> Your **ultimate success** will be when you're no longer needed.

As the SOAR instigator and cheerleader, your ultimate success will come when you're no longer needed. You're working hard to put yourself out of a job. This may seem contradictory, but your goal is not to bind your children and their efforts so closely to you that they are never free to fly on their own. Getting back to our flight analogy, you're flying now so they'll fly later. In order to ensure this, it's vital you pass along this final concept of *responsibility*.

Over the next several chapters, we're going to look at responsibility from a whole-person point of view—in other words, at physical responsibility, emotional responsibility, relational responsibility, and spiritual responsibility. God is sovereign over every aspect of our lives, and healthy children internalize this truth in order to grow up into healthy adults.

Responsible for My Body

Let's talk first about physical responsibility. After all, we live within the physical bodies God gave us. Sadly, our children's physical bodies are being compromised by unhealthy habits and practices. We've looked at your child's activity level as it relates to physical play and movement. We need to be as physically capable as we can so that when God calls, we're ready to respond. An overweight, underfit body has a difficult time responding to tasks with energy, optimism, and enthusiasm.

In order to prepare our bodies to participate physically in the world, we also need to use the right type of fuel. Our bodies need proper nutrition to operate optimally. If the body is not properly fed, it just won't respond well, and that tends to adversely affect other areas. Don't you see this in your own life? If you're not feeling well physically—if you're tired, sluggish, or weak—it's difficult to be upbeat emotionally, have good relationships with others, and feel connected spiritually to God. Face it: it's a struggle to *do* good when we *feel* bad!

> It's a struggle to do good when we *feel* bad!

Think about an automobile. What happens when the fuel you put into the car is the wrong type or dirty or of poor quality? The car sputters and shakes, clunks and smokes. The engine becomes gummed up and doesn't operate properly. The exhaust system gets dirty and pollutes the air. Trying to accelerate to get onto the freeway becomes a life or death experience! When your car operates this way, you know what to blame—bad fuel. Knowing the investment you have in your car, you make sure not to gas up at that station again. Now, if you can make this connection for your car, isn't it time you made it for your own body?

It's true: we bear a certain responsibility for feeling bad because of how we choose to care for our bodies. We fill them with high-sugar, high-fat, low-fiber comfort foods that do little to meet our nutritional needs. Not only do we deprive our bodies of good things but then we also ask our bodies to process bad things. In effect, we double-team against our bodies and then run to the doctor to fix things when they break. By instituting common sense and understanding the way God made our bodies to operate, we can move out of this cycle and into greater health.

Note that I've started out talking to you, about you, not about your kids. As the parent or primary caregiver, your food habits and nutritional choices set

Your food habits set the tone for your children.

the tone for your children. If your snacks are always pre-packaged and artificially flavored, your child will not learn to appreciate natural whole foods. If food is offered as a panacea for every childhood disappointment or difficulty, your child will learn to turn to food for comfort. If you face excess weight, high blood pressure, and high cholesterol levels, your child has a greater chance of having to deal with those issues also. What you eat is what they'll eat. How you eat is how they'll relate to food. If you desire for your child to be healthy and have healthy attitudes about food, are you ready to lead the way in your own life?

God-Given, God-Designed

Our bodies are complex systems that God has designed to operate optimally under some pretty straightforward, simple rules, applicable to every child:

- Eat healthy—natural fruits and vegetables, whole grains, lean meats, and dairy products should be the staples of your child's diet.
- Proper supplementation—begin in childhood to set the pattern of taking a good, absorbable multivitamin and mineral formula.
- Drink water—growing bodies need lots of clean, pure water.

- Play hard—physical activity in childhood prepares the body for an active adulthood.
- Rest well—children need good sleep and a soothing, restful environment in which to rest and fall asleep each night.

Remember that for the optimum health of your child, you need to actively partner with a pediatrician, ideally one who appreciates a whole-person approach to wellness. This partnership is invaluable! I realize many people move from place to place or even state to state, which can make health care continuity difficult. If you do not have a primary care physician for your child, I urge you to locate one and commit to regular checkups. Again, this is especially important if your child is significantly overweight and/or underfit. Your child needs medical supervision, and you need emotional and intellectual backup for the positive changes being implemented within your family.

Good Nutrition in a Fast-Food World

Let's get back to our flight analogy for a minute. Only this time think of yourself and your family not in a jumbo jet flying tens of thousands of feet over the earth but in a helicopter skimming, bobbing, and weaving over the surface. There is no autopilot where helicopters are concerned! You've got to be alert and piloting every moment you're in the air. You'll face obstacles to maneuver around, air troughs and wind shears to be aware of. This is seat-of-the-pants flying.

In today's fast-food culture, when it comes to food, your family isn't flying above the fray only to glide in smoothly each night to a home-cooked, healthy meal. No, there are McDonald's, Krispy Kremes, and vending machines around every corner. To teach your family healthy habits takes seat-of-the-pants nutrition. They need to learn how to maneuver around unhealthy choices and be aware of hidden nutritional shears.

Please don't think this means I've never taken my family to a McDonald's, because I have. And my children know what a donut is. However, these items are occasional treats, not the staples of our diets, as my children learn the valuable concept of moderation.

You can't put your family's nutrition on autopilot.

Moderation and wise decision making can be modeled to your children in many ways, one of which is in your food and restaurant selection. You can now order healthier alternatives when choosing a fast-food restaurant. Items can be shared between children. Milk can be ordered instead of soft drinks. A small ice-cream cone can be chosen instead of a sixteen-ounce milkshake. Here are a few other suggestions:

- Instead of grabbing the food from the drive-through, go into the restaurant, sit down, converse, and eat. Take your time to eat rather than making it just one more hurried activity between others. Allow your children's stomachs time to register becoming full.
- If the restaurant has a children's play area, allow your younger children to engage in some activity after eating.
- Choose a chicken selection over a burger.
- Leave on the lettuce and tomato.
- Ask for barbeque sauce instead of mayonnaise.
- Look for fast-food restaurants where you can order alternatives to french fries.
- Try a Subway or other sandwich shop that allows you to control what goes on your order.
- Make a fast-food stop a weekend treat and go to a river, beach, or park to play afterward.

- For yourself, look for a "junior" selection that usually contains everything that would be on a larger sandwich but in smaller portions.
- Split the fries up and order a salad to share as well.
- Choose a variety of fast-food restaurants instead of always choosing a particular one, and teach your children how to maneuver through each.
- Choose ethnic fast food such as Chinese or Mexican. Look for local options instead of national chains where selections tend to be "Americanized." Many ethnic choices incorporate a higher proportion of vegetables and leaner protein than is typical in American fast-food choices.

Within Limits, Not Off-Limits

Remember, children often find the "forbidden" things of this world highly enticing (we adults have similar propensities—see Genesis 3). Rather than declare certain restaurants off-limits, help your children make positive choices within those environments. For the youngest children, you needn't explain your choices: they will eat what you order. Their joy is in the experience, not the food. As children grow, their ability to assert their own choice grows also, and it's important to begin to fill in the "why" to positive and negative selections. For example, french fries taste wonderful, but they are also full of fat and salt, which is not good for our bodies to grow as God intended. A few fries won't harm you, but a lot of fries can, so you'll be best off keeping those fries within healthy boundaries. Soft drinks are a popular choice, but they give empty calories that provide none of the essential nutrients milk provides or the hydrating power of water. An added bonus of including age-appropriate explanations to your children is the immediate reminder to you as you order your own meal!

These choices and the reasoning behind them need to be presented in a positive way; in other words, not as a self-righteous, *we're better than all these other people* way but as a family choice, one that makes you happier and healthier. As Christians, your children will become very familiar with operating outside of societal, secular boundaries on many things. Incorporating biblical principles and faith into positive food and eating choices is just one more way your child learns that God is a caring, active Father, concerned about the welfare of his children. It's another way to exemplify that God knows the number of hairs on their heads and their every thought and is aware of all aspects of their lives, including what they eat.

Bottom line: think within limits, not off-limits. In this way, your children will develop critical reasoning skills and learn to be responsible for their bodies and their choices. Older children are certainly ready to begin an exploration of the miraculous way God made our bodies to work and to work best. You don't need to leave this valuable lesson to the school system! But you may want to get a refresher course in Body Basics 101 from your child's pediatrician, nurse practitioner, or nutritionist. Understanding how the body works is important so you can "translate" that into age-appropriate responses for your child. Look for resources at your local Christian bookstore that explain the physical body from a biblical perspective. Not only will you be gaining information for yourself, you'll be able to provide the answers when asked the "why" questions.

Cleaning Your Palate, Not Your Plate

Our bodies often get very comfortable with what we feed them. Eat junk food, and that's what we'll want. We'll prefer the taste of fat, salt, and sugar over whole grains, fruits, and vegetables. A cookie will taste better to us than an apple. A donut will taste better than whole grain bread.

We've trained our bodies by sheer repetition to accept certain foods and reject others. In short, we've polluted our palate. It no longer has the ability to discern what's *really* good for us.

Many of our children have lost the joy of a crisp, cool apple or the crunch of raw carrots or the texture of whole grain bread. Fresh, clear water has been replaced by sugared, carbonated soft drinks. Think of your child's palate as a flowing stream. When you fill it up with processed, packaged junk food and drink, a toxic spill, so to speak, is wreaking havoc on your child's

> **It's your job to clean up your child's nutritional environment!**

internal ecosystem. As the parent or primary caregiver, it's your responsibility to clean up your child's nutritional environment!

If your child is small, returning to a natural, healthy environment is easier; you'll have less damage to undo. If your child is older or even an adolescent, reintroducing healthier foods and cleaning up that polluted palate will probably be harder—harder, but not impossible, for your advantage with an older child is their cognitive reasoning abilities. They can more easily understand why what they are eating is unhealthy and the reasons for making positive changes.

In order to clear the palate in food or wine tasting, you need to eat or drink something bland to neutralize the old taste so the new taste can stand on its own. At first, your child may feel that what you're substituting is bland compared to the pumped up foods he or she is used to eating. That's okay. Keep providing healthy, nutritious alternatives and reiterate, in a loving way, how these new choices are beneficial.

Many children and teenagers eat what's available. They come home from school hungry and reach for the first thing they can find. Often, taste is secondary to convenience. You can assist yourself in this cleaning-of-the-palate project by providing your child with convenient, healthy snacks and food choices. Instead of buying whole carrots that need to be scrubbed and chopped, buy small "baby" carrots that can be rinsed and eaten immediately. Put small amounts of ranch dressing into one-ounce cups for easy dipping. Here are a few other suggestions to point you in the direction of creative solutions to your child's at-home snacking:

- Buy broccoli pieces instead of whole broccoli that needs to be cut up.
- Instead of ice cream, provide different flavors of low-fat yogurt, preferably with active acidophilus cultures for better digestion. You can even freeze the yogurt to make it a frozen treat.
- Pre-section fruit such as apples, oranges, or grapes, and have it available for your child to pick up and eat. Place in sealable sandwich bags to ensure freshness in the refrigerator.
- Portion out individual servings of applesauce. Sprinkle cinnamon on top or serve warmed in the microwave on a cold day.
- Buy individually packaged low-fat string cheese to provide a protein snack.
- Try a variety of healthy meal bars and find several your child enjoys and will eat. These should be like a 40-30-30 bar, with a balance of protein, carbohydrates, and fat, and not a granola bar or pseudo-candy bar. (We use several types and flavors at The Center. They taste wonderful and are an excellent alternative to a candy bar. For more information, please go to our online store at www.aplaceofhope.com.)
- Pre-make a half sandwich for your child using whole grain bread, vegetables, and lean meat or cheese.

- Keep a pitcher of cold water in the refrigerator along with milk, orange juice, or a cranberry blend juice. (Do not provide soft drinks for snacking. These calorie-rich, nutrient-poor drinks, full of sugar and caffeine, do nothing to promote your child's health.)
- Buy healthy, low-fat, low-sugar cereal—good right out of the box or with milk.
- Pre-make your own trail mix of oatmeal, raisins, nuts, and/or dried fruit and place in single-serving snack-sized baggies.

The key here is to have a variety of options ready and available for your children. As you are helping them clean their palate, you don't want to add barriers to their positive behaviors. If you think that preparing these items ahead of time is enabling, yes, you're enabling them to develop healthy food habits! As your children age, their ability to prepare their own healthy snacks will improve. A word to the wise, however: teenagers are also highly convenience-oriented and may slip into unwise choices if healthy alternatives are not readily available.

Plan for the Transition

Do these suggestions require advanced planning and time for execution on your part? Yes! You must be at least one step, if not two or three steps, ahead of your growing children. Your goal is to provide them with options—healthy options. In this way, they still will have choices, and you will be able to see where potential challenges may lie. For example, you may have a child who will eat fruit but not vegetables. Look then for ways to bundle vegetables with other flavors or foods. Serve carrots with ranch dressing, celery with peanut butter, broc-

Don't be fooled into thinking healthier food is more expensive to eat.

coli with cheese sauce. Try something a little more exotic, like baby sugar beans or dried peas.

During this time of transition, intentionally remove all—yes, all—cookies, candy, ice cream, salty snacks, packaged desserts, and soft drinks. These should not be a snacking option. You'll be providing lots of delicious, healthy alternatives that are convenient to access. You may hear some grumbling at first, but I think you'll be surprised how quickly those others are forgotten, as long as there are plenty of other choices available.

If you are worried about the cost of providing healthy snacks, let me just say this: some of these alternatives will require more money, but look seriously at how much you were spending on the "junk" food and how quickly it tended to disappear. Healthy, nutritious food will fill up your child better and longer. He or she will eat less because what is being eaten is providing needed nutrients. The body won't keep asking for more—more quantity in search of quality. You will probably find you'll actually be spending less and enjoying the food more. Remember, these are for you also!

Three Squares

We've talked about convenience and snacks. Let's switch gears and talk about the three main meals during the day. With some exceptions, most children are on a breakfast, lunch, and dinner schedule. You must provide your child a healthy, substantial breakfast at the start of each day. Active, growing children will need nutrients and energy after having gone ten to twelve hours without food, from evening to morning. Now, breakfast can come in a variety of ways—one of which is through a vitamin-hyped sugared cereal. This is not what I mean by nutrients and energy. Just because a highly sugared cereal says it has vitamins and minerals is not a reason to choose it! Rather, you want your cereals to be whole grain, low-fat, and low-sugar. Often these cereals can be eaten cold in the spring and summer and hot in the fall and winter. For additional hot cereal selections, look for slower-cooking oat or bran cereals. The quicker these cereals cook, the more of the fiber has been taken from them. The longer these cereals cook, the more "natural" they are, with great dietary fiber. Add fruit for sweetness, dairy products for protein. Supplement each morning meal with a good children's multivitamin

> A **nourished** child is ready to succeed in life.

and mineral tablet. Make breakfast count. Not only will it send your child off into the day nutritionally fortified, it establishes a healthy set point for his or her glucose and insulin levels throughout the day. A fed, nourished child is a child ready to succeed at school, play, and just plain life.

Springs of Water

Let's not forget, in this discussion of food, the benefits of water. Your child must drink lots of water during the day, and more the older the child. Children need to develop a "taste" for water. This is very difficult to do if the only liquids being ingested are milk, juice, or soft drinks. Children should have more water than milk, more milk than juice, and more juice than soft drinks, which should only be offered on rare occasions. Part of cleaning the palate is returning to a satisfaction with the drinking of water. It should not be considered the fluid of last resort, to drink only if there's nothing else around.

School Lunches

When I was in elementary school, lunch was a hot, balanced, full meal. Unfortunately, in most school environments currently, often a school lunch doesn't resemble anything remotely nutritious. Fresh fruits and vegetables are lacking.

High-fat foods are often served. As children get older, they are given complete discretion over what they eat, including fast-food type selections of pizza, burgers, and fries.

Unless your child is at an exceptional school, I strongly suggest you send a sack lunch most days. Certainly, you may go over each week's upcoming menu with your child and determine which school lunches are nutritious and appropriate. For the other days, be prepared to send your child to school with a homemade lunch. Allow your child to participate in making his or her lunch, under your supervision, for the following day. In this way, you can talk about the selections, and your child can positively anticipate the following day's lunch. Hopefully, more of the lunch will end up in your child's stomach and less in the cafeteria trash can. Generally, your child's sack lunch will include a nutritious sandwich, a fruit, a vegetable, and milk, which can be purchased at school. Instead of cookies or candy for something sweet, you might put in some trail mix or a half of a meal bar.

> Allow your child to help with his or her own lunch selections and preparation.

I know that many people often put some sort of salty chip or similar snack into their child's lunch. Generally, these are empty calories that only add salt and fat. Instead, I suggest making the sandwich either larger or more substantial by adding extra meat or slices of cheese or vegetable. You might also look for dried fruit or slightly salted, dried legumes as an alternative. Think of your child's lunch as brain food. The calories you send need to count for something toward your child's ability to perform well academically, socially, and physically.

If your child is not yet of school age, these principles still apply. In or out of school, children are in a God-directed growth mode. They need to be properly fed and nourished to reach their divinely-determined potential.

Around the Dinner Table

As a general rule, most nights per week, your children need to eat at home with the family. Hot, nutritious meals with a variety of flavors, tastes, and textures should be the norm. Weekday breakfasts and lunches may not be the most appropriate time for "experiments," but a dinner now and then certainly can be. Introduce new foods, new flavors, new recipes. Try to avoid the *if it's Monday, it must be meatloaf* syndrome. Incorporate not just beef and chicken but also pork and different types of fish. Avoid fried foods, fatty meats, and breaded selections. Make sure to serve at least two vegetables, and not routinely a potato and something else. Remember, you don't have to always serve cooked vegetables. Often children like raw vegetables better.

I think it is fine to serve a small dessert after the evening meal. Low-fat pudding is a great option, as is a small bowl of ice cream. Think about ways to incorporate fresh fruit by making an apple cobbler or berry tart. When thinking of a dessert, try to avoid a reliance on those with hydrogenated oils, such as prepackaged cookies or sweets. Think light, think small portions, think augmenting with fresh fruit. Try to keep the family portions balanced. In other words, the adults shouldn't be seen eating demonstrably larger portions of dessert. You don't want to communicate the idea that you get to eat more sweets as an adult. If anything, we adults could do with eating fewer sweets than a growing, active child!

Remember that your child simply may not be hungry for three meals per day, every day. Offer nutritious food at least three times a day and allow your child to communicate his or her level of hunger. Meals should not turn into control battles, with food as the ammunition. If your child declines to eat at dinner, simply cover his or her plate in case their appetite changes during the rest of the evening. Obviously, children who express no appetite for dinner should not be hungry for dessert. You do not control your child's appetite, but you can control his or her food choices in a positive, loving, supportive way.

Healthy Fat

As you actively engage in strategic nutrition for your child, don't forget the fat. Now, this may seem like a contradiction to what I've said previously, but allow me to define what I mean by fat. I don't mean the hydrogenated, saturated bad fat that clogs arteries and adds pounds. Rather, I mean the healthy, beneficial fats so essential to healthy growth, especially brain development. These fats are the omega-3 and omega-6 fats, found in flaxseed, cold-water fish, and nuts. Your child should not be on a "fat-free" diet. If you eat a well-balanced, whole food based diet, your children will come into contact with the good fats. If in doubt, supplement their diet with an essentially fatty acid blend (such as EPA/DHA) that includes the healthy omega fats. (At The Center, we have such a blend made from cold-water fish, highly purified to remove any heavy metals and without cholesterol. For more information, go to www.aplaceof hope.com and search the online store for "EPA/DHA.")

For more information about "good" versus "bad" fats, I encourage you to go to the website for the federal government's new food pyramid at www.mypyramid.gov. You can enter your child's gender, age, and activity level and receive a personalized "pyramid" with detailed information on calories, food choices, and activity level.

Food Freedom and Responsibility

Does all of this seem like more responsibility and less freedom for you? If you answered yes, congratulations on your honesty! Frankly, it's more convenient to serve your family the pre-packaged, pre-cooked variety of food for dinner and to send money for pizza for lunch. It takes less energy to put sugared cereal and milk on the table than to fix a hot meal for breakfast. You may hear less complaining if the house is full of cookies and pop after school. Before we talk about your child's freedom and responsibility, let's take a minute to talk about yours.

> **Your child's nutritional freedom may mean a loss of convenience for you.**

When you became a parent, you accepted the responsibility and were willing to give up some of your personal freedom to raise your child. You did this out of love. Nothing's really changed. This still requires your acceptance of responsibility and loss of some freedom—and your motivation of love for your child. I fully understand that parents are busy, with so many competing responsibilities and tasks each and every day. On your list, your child must take a place of high priority. All of us have days when work or other obligations draw us away from our children. In order for your family to SOAR, these days must be occasional. You cannot run a healthy family on autopilot for long. Eventually, conditions will adversely affect the plane, and the autopilot will not be able to adjust. Accept that the price of freedom for your family to SOAR is your continued vigilance.

Please recognize that as your family adjusts to these positive changes, the flight will go more smoothly. As your child grows and learns from you these important concepts, he or she will begin to integrate them as part of who he or she is. This is called maturation, and it's your plane's destination, where your children will disembark and start a new journey on their own.

Teenagers are notorious for spending less and less time at the family dinner table. You know they eat, but you're not sure what, where, or when. This reality requires a shift in responsibility, especially food responsibility, from you to them. The goal of SOAR is to prepare your child to make good, positive choices as a teenager, choices that reflect an acceptance of the duality of freedom and responsibility.

Freedom rarely comes without responsibility. Children need to learn this early and often.

> **Freedom** rarely comes without **responsibility**.

In order for your maturing child to comprehend how freedom and responsibility work in a physical sense, they need to appreciate the choices they make over their own bodies. Teenagers are taking more and more control over how they treat their bodies—how they are fed, how they are clothed, which activities they are involved in. Food freedom and responsibility teach a valuable lesson that is transferable to the consumption of alcohol or drugs, sexual activity, self-care, and high-risk behaviors such as smoking, gambling, and even driving.

Above all, children need to understand they have a unique, divinely appointed purpose for their lives that comes from God. The resource of their physical body should not be squandered by poor choices. Children have the right to have positive and negative choices explained, along with their respective consequences, and we have the obligation to explain them. If you have been overweight or underfit from childhood, don't you wish someone would have explained how challenging it would be to change patterns in adulthood? Don't you wish someone would have lovingly guided you to healthier behaviors and gently held you accountable as you grew in them? You can be that someone to your child.

Grace and Responsibility

Allow me, at this point, to warn you again about the dangers of perfectionism and rigid, all-or-nothing thinking. Your child will fail. You yourself will fail. This does not mean that either of you are a failure. Rather, you're a human being, flawed but loved by God and empowered by his Spirit to do better next time, to learn and grow, and, as Romans 12:2 says, to *be transformed*. God could have transformed us instantaneously upon our acceptance of his sovereignty in our lives. He didn't—and he is perfect. Therefore, he has perfect reasons for allowing us to go through this process of transforming and maturing over time, even though it means we fail and falter. If this pattern for you is acceptable to God, it should be acceptable to you for your child.

This is especially true in the area of food, weight, and body image issues. As a counselor who has worked for over twenty years in the field of recovery from eating disorders, I cannot emphasize enough the damage done by parents or caregivers pressuring children with their own demands (verbal and nonverbal) for perfection and worldly standards of beauty. SOAR is not about outward appearance; it is about inward character.

In our outward-obsessed culture, teaching inner values is hard. The charge given to women in 1 Peter 3 is certainly applicable to help you avoid the trap of outward-not-inward emphasis: "Your beauty should not come from outward adornment, such as braided hair and the wearing of gold jewelry and fine clothes. Instead, it should be that of your inner self, the unfading beauty of a gentle and quiet spirit, which is of great worth in God's sight" (1 Pet. 3:3–4). Now, allow me to paraphrase it regarding your children: "Your heart's desire for your child shouldn't be for outward appearances such as how she looks or what he has or what she wears. Instead, it should be for the quality of their inner self, the unfading attractiveness of a strong and confident faith, which is of great worth in God's sight." Don't push physical perfection, or perfection of any kind; it is unattainable and its pursuit is damaging. Rather, emphasize the pursuit of excellence for God in all endeavors, a healthy love for self, and a grateful acknowledgment of grace.

Your job is to get your child firmly established on the right path, remembering that righteousness is not derived from eating this fruit or avoiding that fat. Rather, faith means accepting God's direction and sovereignty over our lives, including our physical bodies, and living accordingly.

Father, I confess I have negatively impacted my child's health. I've been more concerned about convenience and my time and haven't taken the care I need to prepare nutritious food. I've modeled poor food choices myself. I've allowed my own attitudes about weight, food, and body image to damage my child. I confess these things and ask for forgiveness. Help me undo this damage and teach my child about the wonders you've designed into the human body. Let my example now be one of honoring the body I've been given and showing grace and patience to myself and my family. Amen.

7

R Is for Responsible for My Emotions

"In your anger do not sin": Do not let the sun go down while
you are still angry.

Ephesians 4:26

Just as children come in all body types, they also come in
all emotional types. Some children are natural stoics. Some
children have a seemingly endless supply of pendular emotions. Other children are one-sided emotionally, reacting to
a variety of situations with a specific emotional response,
such as anger or disappointment. You may have emotionally different children but one desired outcome—for
each child to become responsible for his or her emotional
responses.

Knowing Your Own Emotional State

Once again, before we begin to talk about your child,
we need to talk about you. As the adult role model, you

need to have your emotional act together. Just as your own poor food choices can make it difficult for your children to eat responsibly, your poor emotional choices can make it difficult for your children to react responsibly. Your emotional stability, or lack thereof, provides an environment for your child's emerging emotions. Think for a moment how you usually respond to the following situations with your child—not what you hope you'll do or what you think you should do but your standard response.

- How do you respond when your child whines?
- How do you respond when your child is excited?
- How do you respond when your child is angry?
- How do you respond when your child is happy?
- How do you respond when your child is defiant?
- How do you respond when your child is hopeful?
- How do you respond when your child is sad?
- How do you respond when your child is right?
- How are your responses to others different from how you respond to your child?

How you respond to your child, and to others, speaks volumes. As the adult, you set the emotional tone for your child, affecting his or her own emotional responses. Let's take a look at each of the previous questions.

When Your Child Whines

How do you respond when your child whines? I thought I'd choose the most personally irritating first! A child whines when disappointed or frustrated—when what he or she wants to happen does not happen. They take on a tone of voice, a look in the eye, even a body stance that's generally unmistakable to you—and any casual observer within twenty feet. Your child's goal in whining is to get what he or she wants, and kids do this because they've learned how irritating this is to you. They'll risk punishment because their shortsighted desire to have what they want outweighs a potential negative reaction.

Many parents find whining one of the hardest states in which to deal with their child. The parent can react with anger and a short temper, which generally causes the situation and the whining to escalate. The more firm you are about your decision, the more frantic your child becomes to change your mind. Usually this situation ends up one of two ways: either the parent gives in and the child "wins" the battle, or the parent furiously reiterates their right of refusal and the child is left even more disappointed, frustrated, and angry. Neither of those scenarios is a positive one.

> Instead of reacting in anger, take a moment to play detective.

Let's look at what could be going on under the surface of your child's whining. Your child may be misinterpreting the negatives of not having what he or she wants. In other words, the disappointment of being told "no" may be triggering other feelings of disappointment or rejection experienced that day. He may have been chosen next to last for a play team. She may have had an argument with a friend. They are already having a lousy day, and being told "no" to that treat or privilege has just sent them over the edge. Now they're really upset and frustrated and they don't care if you know it. They don't care if *everyone* knows it.

How you respond in this situation sets the tone for your child. Instead of reacting in anger, take a moment to play detective:

- Does this behavior occur every time you go to the store? Is this a predictable, checkout line–type battle? If so, you can head this off at the pass by reestablishing your boundaries, in a pleasant but firm tone of voice, before you enter the store or the situation. If this is a recurring pattern, recognize your own contribution to it by your own past behavior. If you've given in, even just occasionally, you've set the stage for your child to consider taking the risk of whining to get what he or she wants.

- Is your child worn out, tired, and just plain grumpy? If so, his or her ability to moderate emotions is compromised by fatigue. Showing a little extra tenderness while still holding your ground can help diffuse the situation. If that fails, recognize that your child needs to go home and rest and try to alter any plans accordingly. Pushing a tired child to go one more place, do one more thing, is a recipe for frustration all around.

- Is your child trying to communicate an unanticipated need? As adults, we have a hard time remembering that children don't think like we do. Their motivations for wanting things can be totally different from ours. The value they place on objects or wishes can seem out of place to us. When we fail to pay attention to these unanticipated needs, we create frustration and anger in our children. This does not mean you must give in. But you should take the time to establish eye contact with your child and ask a few simple questions, such as, "You know this isn't something I usually get for you. Why is it so important for you to have it today?" or "You know we're going over to grandmother's house tonight so you won't be able to play at Tommy's. Is there a reason you need to see him today?" Your child may have bundled this seemingly inconsequential treat or object or privilege with a deeply felt need. The goal, again, isn't to give in but to ascertain the deeper need so you can meet it in an appropriate way.

Teachable Moments

If you have a standard response that goes no further when your child is acting inappropriately, you miss an opportunity for connection and interaction with your child. You fail to provide your child with a way to modify his or her behavior in a positive way, and your child misses a valuable lesson in maintaining personal emotional balance. These moments are teachable moments and, with a little extra care, can be used for the molding and maturing of your child.

Emotional moments are teachable moments; make the best of them.

God does something similar with us and our potential misbehavior. Listen to 1 Corinthians 10:13: "No temptation has overtaken you but such as is common to man; and God is faithful, who will not allow you to be tempted beyond what you are able, but with the temptation will provide the way of escape also, so that you will be able to endure it" (NASB). God allows us to experience temptation and then provides a way of escape for us to take, if we will, so we learn and grow. When your child is misbehaving, the loving thing to do is to stop, connect with your child, and look for a way out. If your child alters his or her behavior, a valuable lesson has been learned. If your child barrels on ahead regardless, consequences will occur, providing other valuable lessons. As parents, we can at least be as gracious to our children as God is to us.

When Your Child Is Excited

How do you respond when your child is excited? Do you take the time to stop and experience his or her joy? Do you jump up and down and high-five? Or do you minimize their reason for excitement and marginalize their joy because it contrasts with your own negative feelings about life?

Can you allow your child to experience victories that have nothing to do with you?

A child's excitement can be time-consuming and inexplicable. It could be over a bug crawling on the floor or an incomprehensible picture. It could be over a victory in a neighborhood sandlot contest or video game. Often children's excitement comes from accomplishments we adults have forgotten or trivialized. When we fail to share our children's joy, we alienate ourselves from them. They can't understand why we aren't happy for them. It sets up a barrier not only for the next time unexpected excitement hits but in our relationship.

Find out what excites your child and you gain a window into his or her soul.

Sharing what your child finds exciting is important. This will tell you a great deal about your child. You need to slow down or even stop what you're doing and take note. Allow your child's joy to invigorate and refresh you. I believe that through our children God gives us the gift of remembering forgotten blessings. After all, when was the last time as an adult you stopped long enough to marvel at the iridescence of a dragonfly's wing? Or to appreciate the ability to transfer intangible thought onto tangible paper? You don't need to analyze and weigh the merits of why your child is excited. Simply share your child's joy. Remember what makes your child excited; you can use it in love later to bring even more joy.

When Your Child Is Angry

How do you respond when your child is angry? Many of us as adults have learned not to whine, but all of us remember very well how to be angry. When our children express anger, we often respond by becoming angry ourselves, and it's rarely righteous anger. Generally, we respond to our children with anger because we're tired, stressed, confronted, frustrated, and out of patience. None of these is our child's responsibility. If we're tired, we need to get more sleep. If we're stressed, we need to cut down on our commitments. If we're frustrated, we need to ascertain why and make adjustments. If we're out of patience, we need to pray.

Let's think about why our children become angry—probably for the same reasons we do. Your child could be tired because he's accompanied you on outings for three nights in a row. Your child could be stressed because she's got a test tomorrow and a band concert tonight. Your child could be frustrated because a parent who was supposed to show up didn't. Your child could be out of patience because sometimes we simply all get that way.

Anger is a powerful reaction to pain, discomfort, or distress. If you can identify the source, you have a way to deal with it. Too many of us deal with our children's anger by blowing up ourselves. In essence we take the flicker of their anger and respond with a flamethrower of our own. We "win" the argument when the heat of our anger fries their resistance to a crisp. Do we get our way in the end this way? Yes, but we leave behind a burned child.

A child's anger generally has a discernable reason. Be patient, dig deep enough, and you'll find it. Your child will be more likely to suspend their reactive response if they are confident you'll listen and help deal with the source of their pain. Your job as a parent is not to control your child's anger but to help your child learn to control his or her own. Galatians 5:23 says that we are to be *self*-controlled. This is not an easy lesson, and your child will need ample opportunities to practice prior to adulthood. Don't shortchange your child's emotional education by refusing to allow your child to be angry or by attacking your child in anger for their anger. Teach your child how to handle their own anger by handling yours.

When Your Child Is Happy

How do you respond when your child is happy? A happy child can be an invisible child—they're happy, so they're not coming to you. Therefore, it's easy to take your child's happiness for granted and fail to acknowledge it. You may think your child *should* be happy all the time; after all, this is the norm you've established for your child. This particular item on your parenting checklist is marked off, so it's on to something else. Let me encourage you to acknowledge and participate in your child's happiness. Compliment your child and take note of any specific thing that makes your child happy. Be aware, also, if negative things appear to make your child happy. For example, a child who is allowed to watch hours and hours of television or eat whatever he or she chooses may be a happy child. Your job as a parent is not to ensure your child's happiness but to provide him or her with ample opportunities to choose to be happy. Don't ignore a happy child, either for good or for ill. Be aware of your child's emotional state, evaluate its source, and acknowledge or intervene as needed.

> Don't let your happy child be an invisible child.

When Your Child Is Defiant

How do you respond when your child is defiant? Anger can be expressed at things; defiance is generally directed at you and is usually accompanied by anger. A defiant child is wrestling with you for control. This control pushes so many buttons. It triggers family patterns and your own childhood experiences. In the heat of the battle, it can be difficult to remember that this defiance is a characteristic of all humans, not just your child. In a contest of wills, your job as the parent is to win. However, it is not to win at any cost. You must win the battle and still win the war over the heart and love of your child.

How do you win both the battle and the war? Your child must be as assured of your love as he or she is sure of your eventual victory. The child who feels he's lost your love has nothing further to lose as far as your relationship is concerned. Why should he moderate his behavior? Why should she acquiesce to your wishes? Nothing is left to safeguard if she feels your love is lost.

A persistently defiant child must be addressed. Ignoring or minimizing a pattern of defiance today can mean even greater defiance tomorrow. Every child will occasionally refuse to budge, intent on their own will, but if defiance is a pattern, I urge you to seek professional help. Allow someone who is trained to come alongside you and coach you and your child on how to move beyond this pattern of defiance. The underlying core issues can be successfully identified and addressed, allowing you to reestablish a healthy, respectful relationship.

When Your Child Is Hopeful

How do you respond when your child is hopeful? Children can be the world's greatest optimists. Each day, they literally learn something new; they grow and change. Life is a grand adventure—why not respond with hope for the future? Only when children are not shown a pattern of love, care, nurture, and support do they begin to lose the capacity for hope. Yet even the severely abused child will retain a dim flicker of hope. Children are truly remarkable.

Adults, on the other hand, can be the world's greatest pessimists. We worry; we remember the bad times and anticipate more of the same. Day after day brings the same struggles with little progress. Sometimes adults feel it is their job to "educate" children on "the way life is." They believe children need to know about the harsh realities of life so they'll be tougher and more resilient. Sadly, the opposite often happens. Children become dejected and demoralized, more vulnerable, not more resilient.

How you respond to your child's expression of hope is extremely important. Do you honor their faith? Do you agree with their optimism? Or do you attempt to "set them straight" by listing all of the reasons to doubt a positive future? If your son tells you he wants to grow up to be a major league ball player, do you support his aspirations? Or do you tell him that few top-notch athletes ever get beyond college level? If your daughter says she wants to be a doctor, do you applaud her choice of a caring career? Or do you explain how many years of schooling are required and how expensive it is?

> **Children are the world's greatest optimists.**

Career aspirations come and go in children—a ball player today, a doctor the next. God's aspirations for your child are eternal and his promises are rock solid; children have every reason to hope in their bright future. Allow your child to SOAR on the wings of hope and believe in the bright future God has planned just for him or her. Be inspired by your child's hope and faith. Nurture it instead of seeking to place it within a confining box of your personal, unfulfilled dreams. And remember, there is hope for you too; with God, we have enough hope to go around!

When Your Child Is Sad

How do you respond when your child is sad? Few things are as heart-wrenching as a child immersed in sadness. I don't mean disappointed or disheartened but truly sad. As I said before, children are natural optimists, so when your child is sad, pay attention. Find out the reason. Take the time to talk to, hug, and comfort your child. Allow your child to express his or her sadness without you trying to make it go away quickly. The hearts of children are tender. They can be wounded by a harsh comment, a shouted order, a friend's rejection, a parent's illness, or a loved one's death.

Some children become sad because they have a greater empathy than others for the pain they see around them. Help these sensitive children understand their important gift of empathy. Teach them how to put their sadness into perspective and balance it with optimism, hope, and joy. Sadness needs to be expressed, examined, and understood, and your child will look to you to help with these feelings. Avoid the temptation to dismiss or truncate sadness. Allow your child to experience it; then place it in context with God's love and joy.

When Your Child Is Right

How do you respond when your child is right? Children are sometimes the ones in the right when disagreements occur with their parents. We parents make mistakes. We say things we shouldn't. We make rash decisions and expect our children to abide by them, even when they don't make sense. We can think more of our own interests than the interests of our children. When this happens to you, can you apologize to your child? Can you take responsibility for being wrong and ask for forgiveness?

If you never apologize to your child when you're wrong, how can your child come to you when he or she messes up? If you refuse to ask for forgiveness when it's clearly needed, how will your child feel about asking for your forgiveness? What does your reticence say about pride? You do not, as a parent, need to pretend to never make a mistake. You do need to model to your children the value of forgiveness. If they don't learn it from you, how will they understand and appreciate the forgiveness of God? Reject personal pride and the deceptions of perfectionism. Accept your fallibility and teach your children the value of forgiveness and the unbreakable bonds of family.

Family Responses

How are your responses to others different from how you respond to your child? Examine whether you respond differently to others than you do to your family. You don't want to be two-faced where your family is concerned. What are you telling your children if you are the model of patience with others but short-tempered at home? How will your children interpret your actions if you are attentive and calm with them in public but distracted and frazzled with them at home? If you would be embarrassed by your behavior in front of others, why are you not embarrassed in front of your own family? They deserve to see you at your best. Granted, each of us falters and acts inappropriately around our children in private. But if we can control ourselves in public, we should be able to control ourselves in private. Our children deserve our love and respect, no matter who else is watching.

> Don't save the worst of your behavior for your family.

Emotional Stability

In *Raising an Emotionally Intelligent Child*, Dr. John Gottman cautions against three types of parenting styles: dismissing parents, who marginalize their children's emotions; disapproving parents, who are critical of their children's emotions; and laissez-faire parents, who accept whatever emotions their children display but set no limits for those displays. None of these styles positively integrates the natural emotions of children into healthy parenting. If you dismiss your children's emotional states, you dismiss your children, and your ability to influence them diminishes also. If you constantly express disapproval of your children, you crush their spirit. They will either reject you or rebel against you. If you adopt an "anything goes" attitude toward your children's emotions, you deny them the opportunity to learn to regulate their emotional states. None of these teaches your child emotional responsibility.

> **Don't be afraid of your child's emotions; be alert to what they say about your child.**

Children need to test out their emotions. They need to experience them, express them, and learn to deal with them. How you react emotionally is being observed and factored into this amazing learning process. I have dealt with innumerable people who were shut down emotionally by their parents as children. These individuals struggle for years and must retrace their childhood steps in order to get back on the right path emotionally. I have also dealt with people who were taught by example to express whatever emotion they felt in whatever way they chose. Their family and friends generally find them to be unsafe and abusive. These individuals also must learn anew how to relate to other people.

Don't be afraid of your children's emotions. Be alert to them, learn from them, and model back to your children healthy emotional responses. Ask God to help you personally integrate and model emotional responsibility.

Pick Your Battles

Not every emotional outburst by your child is reason for in-depth therapy. Not every tear is cause for concern. Children are different and will react to situations differently. All children, however, should go through a wide range of emotions. They should be happy, sad, defiant, hopeful, whiny, excited, angry—and much more. As opportunity arises, help your child navigate these emotions, especially those that are strongly felt. These are teachable moments—your child can learn from you, and you can learn about your child.

> Not every tear is cause for concern, but continual tears are.

Be aware if your child seems stuck in a certain emotional state, especially a negative one. It is normal for children to be sad, but not for weeks on end. It is normal for a child to be whiny, but not as a persistent reaction to life. It is normal for children to express anger, but not repetitively or by lashing out to hurt others.

If you suspect a problem, call for backup. Speak to your pediatrician or your child's teacher, who will be aware of what's "normal" for children that age. Seek out a professional counselor or child mental health specialist if the problem persists or is resistant to your attempts to bring about improvement. This isn't an admission of failure; it's an acknowledgment that others can be brought in to help in this important area.

Father, thank you for making us as diverse emotionally as we are physically. Help me to know and understand my child's emotions. I confess I've allowed the sun to go down on my own anger. I accept that my emotional stability is a model for my child. Help me to allow my child to experience and express emotions. Alert me to any difficulty my child has with emotional stability, and help me to subdue my pride in order to get needed help. Amen.

8

R Is for Responsible for My Relationships

Honor your father and your mother as the LORD your God has commanded you, so that you may live long and that it may go well with you in the land the LORD your God is giving you.

Deuteronomy 5:16

Hand-in-hand with emotions come relationships, for relationships are formed and forged on the anvil of emotions. No matter the age of your child, he or she is currently in relationship with you and others in your family. When children are little, parents tend to shepherd them through their relationships, but this influence begins to dissipate as the child grows. We've spoken about younger children quite a bit, so let's take a moment to highlight teenagers.

Teenage Relationships

Those of you with teenage children may be nodding your heads enthusiastically at this topic of relational responsibility. After all, your children are developing their own friends—often inexplicable to you! You're concerned about the influence of their friends and about potential sexual activity. This area of relationships for those with teenagers is a minefield, fraught with both anticipated and hidden dangers.

You have a right to be concerned. Proverbs talks about friends in this way: "A righteous man is cautious in friendship, but the way of the wicked leads them astray" (Prov. 12:26) and "Do not make friends with a hot-tempered man, do not associate with one easily angered, or you may learn his ways and get yourself ensnared" (Prov. 22:24–25). Friends have influence over us. Teenagers especially tend to be "pack animals" and adopt the attitudes, beliefs, and values of the group with whom they associate. Pointing this out to teenagers can be a dicey proposition, as they tend to cling quite tightly to the image of defiant independence. Take, for example, teenage styles of dress, hair, or ornamentation. Teens adopt these styles as a way to declare personal independence, without taking into account their desire to fit into a group mentality. This paradox is visible to you, as the adult, but not necessarily to your teen.

> Teenagers tend to be pack animals, all the while stoutly defending their individuality.

The teenage years are a time of personal formation; your teen is making decisions about what sort of a person he or she wants to be. That is why it's vital he or she has been given the tools needed to navigate these tricky waters. These tools aren't handed to your children at fourteen, fifteen, or sixteen. Rather, over the course of their childhood, these tools are given, refined, supported, and encouraged. Relational responsibility should be taught from infancy in order to support positive choices in adolescence and beyond. However, it is never too late to start teaching and modeling these concepts. Teenagers are still teachable and will listen to loving, commonsense advice. If your children are young, begin to teach these principles now. With solid grounding, your child can better weather the inevitable storms of adolescence, especially in the realm of relationships.

Salt and Light

As Christians, your children need to understand their role as salt and light in the world. While these lessons are placed in terms of concrete things, they have everything to do with people and relationships. Jesus tells us in the Sermon on the Mount how to view our relationships with other people. He tells us to take the lead in those relationships, not become compromised by them: "You are the salt of the earth. . . . You are the light of the world" (Matt. 5:13–14). Salt and light are *distinctive* and *noticeable*. We are to be out front in our relationships with others, affecting those relationships for good and for God. Further, we are cautioned in Matthew 5:13 not to allow our saltiness to lose its vitality, for if we do, we are "no longer good for anything." In Matthew 5:15 we're reminded that our light is to shine in order to bring "light to everyone." This is the essence of our relational responsibility and what we must model and teach to our children.

I believe we do this by emphasizing the positive. In other words, give your children a firm belief in their own self-worth, in their ability to make good decisions, and in their destiny—as children of God—to have a positive influence in this world. Being salt and light is a God-designed destiny for our children; they can be sure of it and rest in it. Again, salt and light are distinctive and noticeable because they stem from God as their source. God provides our saltiness, and we reflect the light of Christ.

I Like Me

Often children are overwhelmed by peer pressure and lack of self-esteem. One of the fundamental relationships your child must be comfortable with is his or her relationship to self. Emotional responsibility ties in directly to relational responsibility, as it relates to your child's sense of self. A happy, confident child likes who he or she is. This child understands the concept of grace personally and extends it to others. One of your core tasks as a parent is to make sure your child's self-relationship is not compromised by his or her relationship with you. As your child grows, you need to accept and nurture a shift in responsibility from you to your child. In this way, your child becomes gradually more responsible for the relationship he or she has with self.

> Help your child's **relationships** by reinforcing positive messages in your own.

One of the best ways you can support a healthy self-relationship in your child is by conveying positive, life-affirming messages of love, acceptance, growth, and personal responsibility. You must avoid conveying a constant drone of disapproval, distrust, and negativity. Your messages become the "tapes" that will play inside the mind of your child for years to come, if not their entire adulthood. What sort of tapes do you want your child to hear over and over again in your voice?

Take out your journal for a moment and come up with ten affirming phrases you want to give your child as a gift in order to encourage a healthy self-relationship. These are positive truths you believe about your child that you want to pass on. Try to condense them down into concepts or phrases that you can begin to integrate, in a natural way, into your conversations with your child. For example, one of your positive affirmations might be "I believe my child cares about the needs of others." As you speak to your child about their siblings or friends, you can communicate this belief. You might say something like, "You make a wonderful friend." Or one of your positive affirmations might be, "I trust my child to do the right thing." As your child tells you about the struggles and challenges their day presents, you can communicate "You have great instincts, so trust yourself." Take the time to think about and write down these affirming beliefs about your child. Use them; integrate them; reinforce them. Allow your child to become strengthened by your love and faith, even when you are not physically present. Don't underestimate the power of your words to your child!

Circle of Family and Friends

From the springboard of a positive self-relationship, children are ready to expand their relationships out to friends, family, and acquaintances. Each relationship comes with common and unique responsibilities. We are to treat each other in a loving, compassionate way. God expects this of us not only for those people we get along with but also for those we don't. Jesus says in Matthew 5:43–44, "You have heard that it was said, 'Love your neighbor and hate your enemy.' But I tell you: Love your enemies and pray for those who persecute you." Love and prayer are to be the common threads in all of our relationships. Often, children are best at this task; they love easily, forgive quickly, hope endlessly. Children value relationships.

Children have special responsibilities within the relationships God has designed for them. For example, children have a responsibility to obey within their parental relationship. Ephesians 6:1–3 says, "Children, obey your parents in the Lord, for this is right. 'Honor your father and mother'—which is the first commandment with a promise—'that it may go well with you and that you may enjoy long life on the earth.'" As a parent, you must help your children fulfill this commandment so they do not miss out on blessings reserved by God. Do not make it difficult for your children to obey and honor you—make it easy by your loving, caring, compassionate attitude expressed daily.

Sibling Rivalry

Children need to develop positive relationships with siblings and extended family. If your child is a brother or sister to others, you must help him or her understand that loving begins at home. This can be difficult because of an unfortunate reality called *sibling rivalry*. This has been true from the beginning—just read again the story of Cain and Abel from Genesis chapter 4. Few things are more exasperating to a parent than to be in the middle of feuding siblings. The question in a situation such as this becomes *what is the true source of the feud*? Be prepared for the answer to come back squarely in your corner. Sibling rivalry often has its roots in an inequity—either real or perceived—in parental love, affection, or treatment.

In your journal, list your children and the responsibilities and privileges given to each. Ask yourself these questions:

- Is one child given greater privileges than another?
- Is one child given greater responsibilities than another?
- If so, what is your reason?
- If so, what is each child's perception of the reason?

- Has a younger child benefited from your experience with an older child and thus been granted privileges earlier?
- Has an older child been given greater responsibilities because of the presence of a younger child in the family?
- Has one child been given greater privileges, attention, or reward because of a special talent or gift?
- Has one child been given greater responsibilities because of gender?
- Has one child been given greater attention because of negative behavior and need for parental oversight?

You are looking for areas of disparity—where your child may perceive he or she is not being treated equally because of circumstance, temperament, or parental bias. These must be immediately addressed! Your children will find it much more difficult to love and care for each other if sibling rivalry has its basis in actual behavior or an established parental pattern. Be honest with yourself and determine whether you are able to correct this disparity yourself or need to call in some help. If you recognize an unequal pattern but realize it stems from your own family or past issues, I encourage you to seek out a caring professional to help you work through these issues. Get help for yourself so you can overcome any biases surrounding your children. Look for Christian parenting books that target your particular issue. Become informed and make changes so your children can be free to express their loving nature to self, siblings, and others.

Practicing Parity

During this exercise you may have recognized that the disparate pattern comes primarily not from you but from a spouse or another caregiver. As the person who sees the problem, you have the responsibility to address it, even if it originates elsewhere. Lovingly bring your concerns to the other person or persons. Reiterate the damage this does to the family and look for ways to support them in positively addressing this issue. For the sake of your children and your family, don't be deterred in your determination to see equality and parity practiced in your home. The Lord does not practice partiality in his love for us; we should act the same. In the book of Job we are warned of God that "He would surely rebuke you if you secretly showed partiality" (Job 13:10). And we are told in 1 Timothy 5:21 to "do nothing out of favoritism."

> A child who is harder to love should never be loved less.

Now, I understand that some children are simply harder to deal with—even to love—than others. It may be because of their attitude, behavior, or temperament. Yet this does not give us a reason to love them less. Remember that our example is God, who "causes his sun to rise on the evil and the good, and sends rain on the righteous and the unrighteous" (Matt. 5:45). I dare say that each of us—at times—is considered by God to have a terrible attitude, outrageous behavior, and a lousy temperament, yet his love never fails. You must communicate this steadfast, godly love to your children so they can learn to express it as well in your family.

Mentor and Monitor

As your child grows, he or she will come into contact with more and more people outside your family and circle of friends. They will meet coaches, teachers, other parents, other children, other adults. They will encounter mentors and those they simply don't like very well. In all of these relationships, your child is responsible for treating each person with as much dignity and respect as possible. As an adult, you have the responsibility to monitor these relationships in order to provide learning opportunities and to protect your child from harm.

This is a delicate tightrope. You want your child to respect and respond to others, but you don't want his or her safety compromised. You want your child to understand the faith and beliefs of your family, but you don't want him or her to develop a condescending, self-righteous attitude. You want your child to experience and explore the world around, but you don't want him or her to be led astray by unbiblical principles and beliefs. You must act as a mentor and a monitor for your child. The relationship you have with your child must allow him or her to be able to come to you with the particulars of these budding relationships so you can provide guidance and exert control, where necessary.

> **Avoid acting as referee in your child's relationships.**

Again, pick your battles. It's not up to you to act as referee when your child is playing with other children. Rather, keep your ears open and be aware of the tone of play. Intervene only if your child is unable to resolve difficulties with other children on his or her own. Give them a chance to do so, for a time will come when you will not be present and they will need to know how to handle these situations with other children. This is called *socialization*, and all of us must go through it to become positively interacting adults. Wonder how to handle a situation? Ask a trusted friend or a teacher. If a problem persists with a certain playmate, go to that child's parent and come up with a positive strategy involving both children. Don't act too quickly, but don't fail to act if necessary.

For your child to SOAR in life, he or she must develop discernment in relationships. All of us want our children to grow up with lasting, satisfying friendships that teach the value of loyalty, respect, and affection. I hope you can think back to positive childhood friends. What did they teach you about yourself? How have those friendships shaped the person you are today? Recognize that the very same thing is happening right now, today, with your own children.

Leaven

This brings us to another important scriptural concept, that of leaven. Leaven is essentially the yeast that causes the dough of bread or baked goods to rise. Leaven is an agitator; it is active and alters what surrounds it. A little bit of yeast is all that's needed to cause an entire cake or loaf to rise up. The Bible warns about the power of leaven within relationships.

In Matthew 16 and in Mark 8, Jesus speaks to his disciples about the negative "yeast" of the Pharisees and the Sadducees, the religious leaders of that day. Now, you would think their leadership would be a good thing. After all, they taught the people and oversaw the religious activities, many of which were set out in Scripture. But Jesus understood that within the structure of positive relationships can come negative influences. You will want to look for "yeast" even within your child's seemingly beneficial relationships. Look for that friend who elevates himself by putting your child down. Look for that teacher who gains cooperation by yelling or verbal put-downs. Look for that family member who repeats negative messages about your child. In order to safeguard your child, be prepared to alter the relationship.

Teenage Yeast

Let's look again at teenagers. The danger that leaven will inculcate itself into your child's life is greatest during the teen years. Your teen is looking more and more to outside relationships for validation and direction. He or she is developing an inner core that will shape who they become as adults. Because of circumstances—school, activities, jobs—your teenager is coming into greater contact with the world at large. Not everyone in the world will have your child's best interests at heart. Quite frankly, some will desire the opposite. Your teenager heads out into a world where he or she is confronted with the temptations of alcohol, drugs, sexual promiscuity, dishonesty, and addictions of various kinds.

> **Don't abdicate your role as parent merely because your child's age is in double digits.**

So how do you provide your child with safety? Refuse to abdicate your role as parent merely because your child's age is in double digits. Be alert to the moods and circumstances of your child. Be aware of your child's friends and influences. Ask questions and expect honest answers. Don't assume your child is perfect. Be approachable. Be accessible. Be honest yourself. *You* be the safe place your child can come to when the world threatens.

We are to model Christ in our relationships. Children can do this, as well as teenagers. You do it first and show the way. Teach love, kindness, compassion, and forgiveness. Show your children how to balance love of self and love of others. Positively encourage and motivate your children in their relationships. Make sure your relationship with your child is a safe one to come home to.

Father, my most important relationship is not with my child—it is with you. Help me strengthen our relationship so I can strengthen my relationship with my child. I thank you for each child you have given me. Guide me in those relationships. When things get rocky, help me not to abandon those relationships but to cling even more tightly to them and to you. Allow my life to model healthy relationships for my child. Amen.

9

R Is for Responsible for My Faith

He replied, "If you have faith as small as a mustard seed, you can say to this mulberry tree, 'Be uprooted and planted in the sea,' and it will obey you."

Luke 17:6

We have talked at length about relationships. One paramount relationship will affect every other: your child's relationship to God. In order for your child to truly SOAR into adulthood, he or she must appreciate and grasp hold of a personal relationship with the Triune God—Father, Son, and Holy Spirit. Other things are important, but nothing is more vital. This personal faith will sustain and uphold your child throughout life. Through this faith, as the above verse shows, amazing things can be done. With God's Spirit as guide, your child will progress farther and faster than you could ever cause on your own as teacher.

All of us are spiritual beings. This is why whole-person care must address a person's spiritual nature. The spiritual side of a person is that which has the capacity to look beyond today and hope in tomorrow. It's the part that refuses to believe the worst but holds out for the promise of the future. In recovery, no power is greater than the spiritual. We recognize this, address it, and utilize it for good. You can do the same for your child.

> **If you don't address a person's spiritual nature, you fail to address the totality of the person.**

Not everyone, of course, professes a personal faith, but each of us was designed by God with the capacity for faith. In children, this capacity tends to spill over into other areas. It's why kids are such optimists. At a certain age, however, we can choose to either accept or reject this faith. We have free will to choose to sin and choose to repent. In order to teach your child spiritual responsibility, you want to do everything you can to prepare them for that day of decision.

Model Your Faith

The first thing you can do to help your child is to model your own faith. In 1 Timothy 1:2, the apostle Paul acknowledged his role as Timothy's father in the faith. He did this by allowing Timothy to be privy to the intimate details of his own faith. He wasn't secretive or restrained but instead openly and honestly demonstrated his faith and encouraged Timothy to emulate the good he saw. This is your charge for your children. Be open and honest and encourage your children to emulate the positive in your own life. Be transparent also about the bad, and model to your children how to ask for and accept forgiveness. Your children need the spiritual gifts of a prayer life, a study life, a family life, and a life of service in the Lord. Each will be a tremendous spiritual blessing and will fortify your children for the rest of their lives. Let's look at each.

Through Prayer

Children are natural pray-ers. The prayer of a child pours out faith, hope, and love: faith in a Father who hears, hope for an answer, and the love of a trusting child. Provide opportunities for your children to pray. Many people have found that developing a calendar of prayer is helpful. In other words, choose to pray for specific needs on specific days. As your child grows, their capacity to appreciate and actively participate in these prayers will grow. Make sure to include family, friends, leaders, the lost, the hurting, and the sick. These will teach your child empathy and compassion. Make sure to include current events, where age appropriate. These will teach your child to trust in God for the future. Make sure to include confession and admissions of wrong (again, as age appropriate). These will teach your child forgiveness and transparency. Recognize that within the realm of your child's prayers, God's Spirit is active and working. Prepare to be amazed at what you hear your child express during these times of prayer. God is at work in your child; you will see miraculous glimpses within the window of prayer.

Through the Word

Prayer is not the only forum for connecting with God. The Bible is more than an ornate book kept on a coffee table! It is active, alive, and effective. Hebrews 4:12 puts it this way: "For the word of God is living and active. Sharper than any double-edged sword, it penetrates even to dividing soul and spirit, joints and marrow; it judges the thoughts and attitudes of the heart." This powerful gift of God, Spirit-breathed, should become your child's spiritual companion. Within its pages, God will share his enormity, his plan for your child, his love through Christ, and his victory over death. You can never begin too early teaching your child from Scripture. Ultimately, you will want to transfer your love and reliance upon Scripture to your child. A time will come when you are no longer accessible to your child; God's Word lasts forever and is an inexhaustible resource of knowledge, hope, and insight for your child today, tomorrow, and forever.

Through a Spiritual Family Life

The third gift you can give your child is a spiritual family life. This means involving yourself and your child in a faith community. Simply put, take your child to church. Allow your child to be taught by other godly adults and experience the joys of corporate worship. Strengthen your child with the knowledge that he or she is not alone in their faith. We were made for family—physical family and spiritual family. Don't let your child grow up a spiritual orphan because you will not make your own personal commitment to worship God with a spiritual family.

Through a Life of Service

Lastly, your children need the spiritual gift of a life of service in God. We were made for service and for a purpose. Remember Ephesians 2:10? "For we are God's workmanship, created in Christ Jesus to do good works, which God prepared in advance for us to do." This is your child's true purpose in life, regardless of what he or she does for job or career or avocation. We are God's hands and feet, eyes and ears in this world. I truly believe all of us reach our true joy and potential when we have found the ways God designed us to serve others. My counseling practice is my business; it is also my ministry. When I am actively engaged in this ministry, I feel connected to God and useful to others. God has such a purpose, a specially designated service, for your child.

Did you notice the plurals in the Ephesians 2:10 verse—the "we" and "us"? As 1 Corinthians 12 explains, the context for service in God's kingdom is one of a body: many parts working together to accomplish a common good, with Christ as the head. A foot is not a body. A hand is not a body. Only a body is a body. We function as the body of Christ *together*—in other words, within a church. You are doing your child a spiritual disservice if you perpetuate the myth that you can be an "island" Christian—alone and unto yourself.

> God has a specially designed service for your child.

Overcoming Spiritual Hurt

I understand that you may have experienced hurt at the hands of a church or religious group. Please don't think I minimize that negative experience. However, for the good of your child and your family, you need to take steps to move beyond that painful experience and reconnect with a healthy body of believers. (I heartily recommend you read *Toxic Faith* by Dr. Stephen Arterburn and Jack Felton.) Your children need to learn to navigate their faith within the context of spiritual community, for within this community your child will discover their gifts and purpose. Then, knowing that, your child can actively engage as part of a body to accomplish God's will as he intended.

Holy Ground

I'd like you to think for a moment about the spiritual seedbed you're providing for your child. In the parable of the sower in Matthew 13, Jesus talks about seed that fell in different types of soil: along a path, in rocks, in thorns, and in good soil. The pathway soil was hardened and unprotected, so seed that fell there couldn't germinate in the ground and was easy pickings for the birds. The rocky soil allowed seeds to germinate and grow, but the roots were shallow and couldn't stand up to harsh elements. The thorny soil allowed the seeds to grow, but they were quickly choked out by the dominant vegetation. Lastly, the good soil produced an amazing crop because it contained the optimum conditions for seed germination and growth.

What type of soil are you providing for your child's spiritual growth?

What type of soil are you providing for your child's spiritual growth? Is it a soil packed down hard, where seeds of faith can hardly take root and are vulnerable to hungry opportunists? Is it a soil full of the rocks of other priorities that allows faith to flower but makes sustaining that faith a frustrating task of trying to grow in and around other activities and obligations? Is it a soil full of thorns, where faith is permitted but crowded out by negative attitudes and verbal messages? Or is it a good soil, rich in spiritual nutrients and cleared of spiritual obstacles, which will allow your child's faith to flower and blossom, to put down deep roots and multiply?

Encourage Spiritual Gifts

In your journal, I want you to write down at least one positive way you can encourage each of these spiritual gifts—a prayer life, a study life, a spiritual family life, and a life of service—in the life of your child. Make a plan to integrate these into your family life within the next month. Is it a nightly time of prayer? Start tonight! Is it an age-appropriate Bible study? Go to your local Christian store or to your church and get an appropriate resource. Are you between churches? Make a list of places to call, then choose one to visit each week. Is it involving your child in service? Look for ways to help another person in your neighborhood this week and choose a church ministry to participate in with your child.

As Christians, we want our children to develop a mature faith in God. Yet oftentimes we are lazy and look to others to accomplish this for us, giving excuses of too little time, knowledge, or energy. Show your child spiritual responsibility in your own life. Nurture the "good soil" in your family life that will give the seeds of your child's faith the greatest opportunity to grow and flourish.

God's Reward for Responsibility

Simply put, in all these areas of responsibility, you set up the pattern for your child. Scripture even promises, "Train a child in the way he should go, and when he is old he will not turn from it" (Prov. 22:6). Your child needs to internalize this good news that his life has meaning and purpose in God's kingdom. God has made your child to be supported, optimistic, active, achieving, and responsible. God has made your child to SOAR!

Father, you know how much I love my child. Help me to love more. Help me to love like you. I want to model physical, emotional, relational, and spiritual responsibility for my child. Teach me in each area, Lord! Support me so I have the strength to acknowledge my weaknesses. Allow me to look to you for strength. You know my child's heart. Help me to learn about my own child from you. Be with me and with my child each day. Amen.

10

SOAR-ing above Special Circumstances

> For nothing is impossible with God.
>
> Luke 1:37

My hope is that all along, through reading this book, you've been saying, "Yes, yes!" This information based on a common-sense, biblical perspective should resonate within you. None of it is controversial or earth-shattering; rather, it may be what you already know but just need support and encouragement in doing. I applaud you for your efforts on behalf of your family's health!

I recognize also that some of you are reading this and saying, "Yes, yes—but . . ." In other words, you feel the information is generally valid, but you have a particular situation that makes applying these principles challenging. Please don't be disheartened! Remember, "nothing is impossible with God" (Luke 1:37). No matter your circumstance, God is able to help you implement positive, healthy changes in your family.

Nonparticipating Family

With so many families working full time in today's society, children are often in the care of the larger family—ex-spouses, grandparents, or extended family. A circumstance may arise where those assisting in the care of your children do not agree with or acquiesce to the concepts of SOAR. They may not want to invest the time and energy. They may not have a personal faith. They may resent your input into how the children are treated. Let's take a look at each of these.

> **Don't let another person's reticence derail your good intentions.**

One of the hallmarks of SOAR is a commitment by the adult caregiver to adopt these concepts on a personal level. All along, you've been asked to examine your own heart, mind, and soul to determine what barriers or obstacles you are erecting to your family's overall health and well-being. This is not an easy task, and some family members helping care for your children may choose not to engage in this level of self-examination. If this is your situation, please don't allow their reticence to derail your good intentions.

An Ex-Spouse

In the case of an ex-spouse who has shared custody, your ultimate goal is to persuade this person how beneficial the SOAR concepts are to your children. Start first by giving a copy of this book to your ex-spouse. Perhaps you could write a short note explaining how you've found it valuable and expressing your commitment to following its recommendations. In short, declare your intention to SOAR and encourage your ex-spouse to join you for the good of your children. In some ways, you are throwing down the gauntlet of care and concern. Allow your ex-spouse time to read over the book and come to his or her own conclusion.

If your ex-spouse chooses to reject either your offer of the book or the concepts within the book, don't give up! Pray diligently for a change of heart. Work just as diligently to create the SOAR environment in your own home as a buffer and haven for your children when they are with you.

Children are always best off when ex-spouses work together for their good. In the real world, this doesn't always happen, as envy, strife, and division can continue long after the marriage ends. Such a divisive relationship is devastating to children. I urge you to do whatever you can to try to be at peace with your ex-spouse. When you present SOAR, guard against appearing condemning or self-righteous. Plead and exhort from the platform of your mutual love and concern for your children. Don't allow SOAR to turn into just one more contest between you. Attempt at all possible times to work cooperatively together. Determine ahead of time to think positively about this joint endeavor and about your ex-spouse. Allow your ex-partner to rise to the occasion—for the good of your children.

Sadly, for a small percentage of you, this won't be possible. Your ex-spouse will be combative, hostile, and noncooperative. Your options will be limited, so you'll need to take advantage of every one you can. Continue to be as supportive as possible with your children in the home environment you control. Be accessible for your children to bring you their needs and desires. I urge you to resist any temptation to denigrate your ex-spouse. Choose instead to emphasize your own love, care, and concern for your child. Reinforce your commitment to providing a stable,

> Create a SOAR buffer zone in your own home.

loving home. Pray for God to grant your child the wisdom to understand and appreciate the positive environment you're actively creating for his or her good.

We've talked before about the goal of transferring these principles into the heart of your child. The deeper you can prepare the soil of your child's heart, mind, and soul through SOAR in your own household, the greater resilience your child will have when apart from you. Allow your child to experience and grow in these concepts, and then trust in God to protect and remind him or her when needed.

Prepare your child when you are together to be resilient when you are apart.

In short, if your ex-spouse will not support you in SOAR, you will need strength and resolve to carry out the necessary changes without his or her backup. If your ex-spouse is so oppositional now, this is probably not a new situation for you. Use what you've learned in the past—about him or her and about yourself—to guide you this time. Remember, this isn't just about the here and now; it's also about tomorrow. Help your child to SOAR even in these difficult circumstances! My prayer is that when tomorrow comes, you'll receive this reward, found in Proverbs 31:26–28: "She speaks with wisdom, and faithful instruction is on her tongue. She watches over the affairs of her household and does not eat the bread of idleness. Her children arise and call her blessed." In the absence of support from an ex-spouse, please know that you are on the side of the Lord, who desires for your children to grow in wisdom, knowledge, and truth. Let the truth your children internalize about you be your support of and devotion to their well-being.

Grandparents

Many working parents are able to place their children in the care of either their parents or their spouse's parents.

This is a both blessed and challenging situation. Grand-parental care can be convenient and is often less expensive than other alternatives, but the environment your children are going into must take precedence over every other consideration. I'm going to assume that if your children are being cared for during part of the day by grandparents, you've already weighed the advantages and disadvantages to your children and have made the appropriate decisions.

As you integrate SOAR into your home, you will naturally expect that your desires will be honored by the grandparents. My children receive support, care, and nurturing from my parents, which is a blessing beyond calculation. Something is uniquely comforting about seeing your parents love and care for your children. It affirms the love you remember as a child and provides you with your own backup and support as you're raising your children. So don't sell these grandparents short! Sit down and explain what you're hoping to achieve in your family and the positive changes you're implementing. Elicit the grandparents' aid in extending these concepts into the time your children are with them. Give them this book with your endorsement and commitment. Many of this older generation will understand and support these changes, as they in many ways mirror what might be considered "old-fashioned" values.

> **Grandparents can be a tremendous blessing in helping your family to SOAR.**

As a support in the area of food, provide your children with the appropriate meals or snacks to eat while in the care of their grandparents. This will ensure that at least part of what they're eating is approved! It will also relieve these older caregivers from preparing food for your children every day. If the grandparents enjoy meal preparation, work with them on acceptable and unacceptable choices, always providing good, solid nutritional reasons why. Whenever possible, make compromises. If grandmother loves to serve freshly baked cookies twice a week when your children come in from school, limit the number of cookies served with a suggestion to include freshly cut fruit wedges.

People say the acorn doesn't fall far from the tree. Children are often very much like their parents in temperament, physicality, and behaviors. This dynamic can alter significantly, however, if, after the acorn has fallen from the tree, it encounters the living God! Some of you will have found faith in God after you left home, and your children's grandparents may not honor or even understand your reliance on spirituality. If this is the case, do not be ashamed of expecting that your faith—and the faith being passed down by you to your children—be honored in your parents' home. As you speak with your parents about the concepts in SOAR, don't shrink from its biblical basis. Even for those without faith, these concepts are true and rooted in common sense. Who knows? Perhaps through these concepts, your parents may come to understand and appreciate the value of your faith. Remember Jesus's words in John 6:39: "This is the will of him who sent me, that I shall lose none of all that he has given me, but raise them up at the last day." God is at work in this world—in you, in your children, and in your parents.

> **Don't apologize for expecting your faith to be honored.**

Extended Family

Just a word here about extended family—cousins, uncles, aunts, siblings—who might be caring for your children when you are not able to. This situation works when it works for your children. Their well-being must be your primary guide in whether or not this care situation continues.

As in the other family situations, give extended family the benefit of the doubt. Share with them what you are doing in SOAR and why. Give them a copy of the book, and demonstrate your commitment by living out the concepts in your own life. Make your own household a SOAR household, and invite them to follow suit.

Read over again the above section on grandparents with extended family in mind, for many of the ideas apply. Adults can feel uncomfortable insisting on a different style of care from their parents than they received. This shouldn't be the case with extended family. Their help is wonderful, but insist that your parental direction be honored by those caring for your children. Assist where you can by providing meals and snacks. Find out about activity opportunities in their neighborhoods. Investigate whether or not any other children in that household would benefit from these activities. In some cases, offer to pay for their children to participate in exchange for transportation to and from. Find ways to collaborate. Be generous in your support of *their* support of you and your family!

> **Your parental direction must be honored by those caring for your children.**

With any of these care situations, share as much as you're able about the positive environment—emotional, relational, physical, and spiritual—you desire for your children. As you contemplate your presentation, remember the admonition from Proverbs 12:18: "There is one who speaks rashly like the thrusts of a sword, but the tongue of the wise brings healing" (NASB). You need collaboration, cooperation, and support, so choose your words and your actions wisely:

- Communicate your personal commitment.
- Expect and anticipate their support.
- If this support is not forthcoming, fortify your own commitment and, where appropriate, examine other care options.
- Be supportive by preparing meals and snacks yourself.

- Investigate activity options for your children and/or others.
- Be accessible to your children so they can share their other-care experiences, especially as it relates to what you're teaching in your own SOAR household.

Extended Care Situations

If your child spends several hours a day in a day care situation, this doesn't mean you have to abandon SOAR during those times. Rather, you will need to communicate your expectations and desires to your paid caregiver, whether in a private home or institutional setting. Again, be prepared to find allies. Many day care situations require a structured, respectful, even nutritional environment in order to care for a multiple of children. If your day care has a written set of guidelines, read it over and note similarities to SOAR concepts. Also be sure to note anything in direct contrast. These issues will need to be addressed with your day care provider.

> Avoid care situations **hostile** to your faith.

Whenever possible, try to find a day care setting where your family's spiritual values are respected, if not shared. Your children are exposed enough to a secular environment. Anytime you can place them in a Christian environment, all the better! If the situation is not overtly Christian, look for a day care that is neutral. Certainly avoid any that are hostile to faith!

Where meals and snacks are concerned, talk to your provider about menus and food items. Many providers know firsthand the consequences of a room full of children and too much sugar! Be on the alert for too many processed meals and too few natural foods, as processed means convenience and could be extremely attractive to providers short on time or help. If you are using a home day care situation, offering to provide your child's meals and snacks may prove to be a necessary commitment on your part.

In a perfect world, every person who came in contact with your child would epitomize SOAR without effort. In a fallen world, you've got your work cut out for you in supervising your child's extended care situations. Remember, you're still the parent and ultimately in charge. Filter your decisions with your child's well-being in mind. If you face a conflict between your convenience and what's good for your child, choose to help your child. You don't have them for very long, really. And undoing a bad decision takes so much longer than celebrating a good one.

Division in the Home

Again, in an ideal world, husbands and wives would agree on all aspects of parental decisions. We would speak as one voice. You may face a situation in your household where you're the SOAR cheerleader and instigator but your spouse refuses to come on board, as we discussed in chapter 1. If your spouse has still not responded to your call to get on board, please be patient and persistent.

Let's look at what the Bible says about an unbelieving spouse and apply it to SOAR. First Peter 3:1–2 says, "Wives, in the same way be submissive to your husbands so that, if any of them do not believe the word, they may be won over without words by the behavior of their wives, when they see the purity and reverence of your lives." As you are implementing SOAR concepts in a household with a reluctant or non-participating spouse, do so quietly, naturally, without bragging or trumpeting each change. Make small changes and allow your spouse to view the positives. Do not demand compliance but rather gain as much agreement as you can. First and foremost, again, is the depth of your own personal commitment to the benefit of your whole family. Be so convincing in your love that your spouse will *see* the benefits without being *told* the benefits. Show your commitment to SOAR and allow the Spirit to win your spouse over. Realize your behavior speaks volumes. Be sure that volume is tuned to the right frequency! Then pray and trust God to act.

Children with Special Needs

Some children have physical, mental, or emotional challenges that may prove to make aspects of SOAR demanding to accomplish. They should not, however, negate the reasons behind or benefits of SOAR. Who should live in a *Supportive, Optimistic, Active and Achieving, Responsible* environment but special needs children? That environment may look somewhat different given the particular challenge, but it can be tailored for your child's situation.

Physical Challenges

If your child is physically challenged, he or she may not be able to engage in a "normal" amount of physical activity. If you are in this situation, I imagine you've already rewritten "normal" for your child. That is prudent and completely appropriate. I suggest you speak with your child's physician or physical therapist or to other professionals involved in your child's care. Collaborate on areas where your child could increase his or her physical activity. Your goal is to maximize your child's physical potential, whatever level that potential points to. Recognize that your child's "activity" level may need to increase by you engaging in most of the activity. In other words, instead of

> Whatever your child's physical potential, seek to maximize it.

your child taking a walk, you can take your child outdoors. If he or she is in a wheelchair, you can do the pushing and allow your child to enjoy the feel of the air, the smell of the grass, and the sound of the birds.

As for the other aspects of SOAR, a physically challenged child needs to be supported by caring adults, optimistic about his or her future, achieving as much as his or her condition allows, and becoming as responsible as possible for him or herself. If anything, your child may pick up and internalize these concepts more quickly than other children because of the maturity and strength gained through living with daily challenges.

Mental Challenges

If your child has mental challenges, his or her ability to integrate these SOAR concepts may be similarly compromised. This does not negate their benefits to your child. In this case, the aspect that may be affected the most is the area of responsibility. Ultimately, your goal is to transfer responsibility from yourself to your child. If your child is not capable of accepting that transfer, in part or in whole, responsibility will of necessity stay with you and those with whom you have shared it. Make sure it stays in good hands by coaching the other caregivers to SOAR themselves. In this way, your child will be surrounded by supportive adults who are optimistic about what your child can achieve and have accepted the responsibility of caring for your child.

Be consistent and persistent in emulating these SOAR concepts. For those children who have mental challenges, your consistency can provide a life pattern eventually internalized. In the meantime, SOAR will give your child loving, supportive stability. Your child can still appreciate and benefit from a pattern of looking at the positive, being as physically active as possible, achieving success in appropriate tasks, and accepting as much responsibility as his or her condition allows.

Signs of an Eating Disorder

As you work with your child to SOAR, strive to communicate acceptance, love, and forgiveness. When perfectionism, criticism, sarcasm, and verbal put-downs are part of a family structure, children can turn to food for control and comfort. For over twenty years, I've worked with those struggling to overcome eating disorders. In most cases, this perverted relationship with food occurs in childhood or adolescence. In many cases, eating disorders occur in families where parents love their children and were trying hard to do the right thing. Their efforts went off track. In order for your family to SOAR to fulfilled, responsible adulthood, you don't want to veer off course due to an eating disorder.

As you implement positive nutritional changes, don't send out the signal that food is an enemy, that eating certain foods is "righteous" and other foods are "sinful." Thinking this way can be tempting, especially as you make different choices about the food you eat and prepare for your family. Listen to Jesus in Mark 7:18–19: "'Are you so dull?' he asked. 'Don't you see that nothing that enters a man from the outside can make him "unclean"? For it doesn't go into his heart but into his stomach, and then out of his body.' (In saying this, Jesus declared all foods 'clean.')" All foods are clean, so don't impose a self-righteous hierarchy; rather, teach the concept of moderation.

The difficulty is not with the food; it is with our relationship to the food. Anorexics turn to a short list of "safe" foods in an effort to gain a sense of control over their lives. Bulimics turn to large amounts of food for comfort and then purge in various ways to expel the guilt. Binge eaters turn to large amounts of food for comfort and satiation. Compulsive overeaters turn to food to comfort life's difficulties. In all of these, food is not the enemy; it is not made "unclean" by the eating disorder. Rather, what has become "unclean" is the relationship with food.

> The problem isn't with food; it's with our **relationship** to food.

As you seek to integrate healthy decision-making where food is concerned in your household, strive to present food as a gift from God, given to us to fuel our bodies for his work. God wants us to enjoy food but not become gluttons. He declares all food "clean" but expects us to make wise choices about what, when, and how much to eat.

So much of your child's understanding of and relationship with food comes from you. After all, he or she observes you each and every day. What you say is not as important an example as what you *do*. Get your own relationship with food in order and allow your children to see God's wisdom through you.

This section is not meant to be a comprehensive discussion of eating disorders. If you suspect or recognize a problem within your family or want to learn more about eating disorders, I encourage you to read my book *Hope, Help, and Healing for Eating Disorders*. (This resource is available through my website at www.aplaceofhope.com.)

Signs of Anxiety or Depression

As you implement SOAR changes in your family, it is natural for family members to exhibit a level of resistance, depending upon age and disposition. If you have a child who appears extremely agitated or worried about what these changes will mean, how they'll be implemented, who will be involved, when each will be done, and why everything should be turned upside down, this is a child to pay attention to. Exhibiting such a high level of anxiety is a warning sign you should take seriously. Children live in a world of adult rules, adult motives, and adult schedules. As such, children are constantly surrounded by the need to make changes and adapt. Some children accept these changes more easily than others.

Pay attention to an overly agitated child.

For those children for whom change is a cause for extreme concern, you will need to alter your approach. You will need to factor in more time for explanation and modeling. Your demeanor and reactions to these changes, as well as those of the other members of the family, are very important. A calm, reasoned, measured pace of change will help this child. Instituting new patterns with concrete reinforcement can also be helpful. For example, if you are working on being optimistic, this child may need to have a physical chart that records and reinforces when he or she expresses positive, optimistic feelings. For the anxious child, knowing what is expected and what are the outcomes and consequences of compliance is extremely important. This child does not respond to a frenetic, frantic, change-in-schedule lifestyle.

You can, however, gradually allow this child to learn how to positively anticipate the future. Often this requires a process of delving into his or her "mental background"—the tape of messages this child has on all the time in his or her head. Usually an agitated or anxious child has a negative tape running, one based upon a fear of the future, insecurity about an outcome, or lack of confidence in him or herself. Much of your work to help this child SOAR will be to help rewrite these negative messages with positive affirmations based upon God's Word, your love and support, and victories you've helped to support in this child's life.

As I've said, children should be naturally optimistic. Everyone has times when it's hard to get excited about life, but this should not be a constant state for children. A withdrawn, apathetic, unenergetic child should be monitored carefully. The younger the child, the shorter this "down" time should be. If your child has shown a disinterest or general apathy for life or prolonged sadness, I urge you to get help. Start with your child's pediatrician and investigate physical causes. If these are ruled out, don't stop there! Look for emotional causes with the help of a child psychologist or counselor.

Conventional wisdom used to downplay the possibility of childhood depression. Unfortunately, this condition is becoming more commonplace among children. The reasons for this are societal and environmental. Our children are exposed to the chaotic, stressful lives of their parents with little buffering or protection. They are also exposed to a polluted world, unkind to those children physically sensitive to the high degree of toxins present. Environmental toxins can contribute to depression. If it lingers, it must be addressed. Your child will not be able to SOAR if he or she is chained down to depression. Work with a healthcare professional to pinpoint any physical causes for behavioral issues.

Behavioral Challenges

Some children are stubborn. They were born with their back arched, their feet dug in, and their chins outstretched. Some people call such a child "strong-willed." If you've got one, "iron-willed" would probably be your description! This child has such a strong sense of how the world should be that any deviation on your part is met with a battle of wills. It can be extremely emotionally depleting and physically tiring for you. Regardless, you need to win these battles, and generally you can with love, persistence, and prayer.

Even stubborn children can be lovingly but firmly brought to your way of thinking, especially if there is inherent "benefit" for the child. Even a strong-willed child can be brought to understand the benefits of SOAR. But when does a child stop being strong-willed and start being defiant? In this contest of wills, a child should never be allowed to become physically violent—to hit or otherwise seek to injure you or himself. If you have a child who has crossed over the line or who seems incapable of acquiescing to family guidelines or rules, this child could have a behavioral disorder. In this case, as in others talked about in this chapter, you may need to call for reinforcements.

> In a battle of wills with your child, you need to win with love, persistence, and prayer.

Calling in Reinforcements

Your family may be your responsibility, but you don't have to meet these challenges alone. God has empowered and gifted people in medical, counseling, and pastoral fields who have the insight, expertise, and ability to help you with your challenging situation. For children with physical challenges or disabilities, these professionals can partner with you to maximize your child's potential and provide you with knowledge and insight into your child's condition. Any caring professional will support your dedication to SOAR, so don't be afraid to ask for help!

For those children with emotional difficulties or behavioral challenges, help is no less needed than if the problem were strictly physical in nature—but help is sometimes harder to ask for. We can feel personally embarrassed to admit, for example, that our child's behavior is out of control. We can feel it reflects poorly on us as parents. Denying the severity of the problem, we think ignoring it will make it go away. But if it's gotten to this point, it's not going away: it must be addressed.

If your child is exhibiting signs of an eating disorder, anxiety, or depression or refuses to adapt to your guidelines and priorities, I urge you to seek professional help for your child and for yourself. Any of these conditions is extremely draining on you as a parent. In order to have the strength, resolve, and endurance you need to safeguard your child, you need to be built up, encouraged, and empowered to "stay the course."

When problems don't go away, they must be addressed.

Take out your journal and detail any particular situation or condition you identified as especially challenging to you as you worked through SOAR. Ask yourself the following:

- Is this an ongoing condition or has it manifested itself recently?
- Have you tried to make it less of a challenge before?
- If so, what did you do? Was it helpful?
- Would something similar be possible now?
- If not, what else can you do to support your child and/or yourself in this situation?
- What existing, known "reinforcements" can you call upon to help?
- Are there any additional reinforcements you can look for in your family, neighborhood, health care community, or faith community?
- If you have identified such reinforcements, what can you do to access them?
- Identify any barriers to accessing them. What steps can you take to eliminate or get around those barriers?

I wish I could say that getting the help you need for your family will always be easy. In reality, often it is not. As a parent, you need to be open about your needs, persistent in finding help, committed to positive steps, and transparent about your own shortcomings. You need to yell "Help!" loudly and often, while doing everything you can to find solutions and strength.

Strength from Above

Our greatest "reinforcement" is not far from us—God is forever at hand. Psalm 16:8 says, "I have set the LORD always before me. Because he is at my right hand, I will not be shaken." It does not say that the *world* will not be shaken; rather, it says that *I* will not be shaken. On this side of heaven, that is often all we can hope for. God has promised it will be sufficient.

If you face difficult circumstances, you may not be able to see great leaps of progress or frequent milestones. Your efforts will require longer amounts of time, increased patience, decreased personal freedom, delayed gratification, and little appreciation for your efforts. With an acceptance of this reality, you become more like God, who since the fall experiences daily these constraints where we, his children, are concerned:

- We require greater amounts of time—"The Lord is not slow in keeping his promise, as some understand slowness. He is patient with you, not wanting anyone to perish, but everyone to come to repentance" (2 Pet. 3:9).
- He must show us infinite patience—"What if God, choosing to show his wrath and make his power known, bore with great patience the objects of his wrath—prepared for destruction? What if he did this to make the riches of his glory known to the objects of his mercy, whom he prepared in advance for glory?" (Rom. 9:22–23).

- He allows us to affect his plans—"So the Lord changed His mind about the harm which He said He would do to His people" (Exod. 32:14 NASB).
- He must wait for the fruition of his plans—"But in these last days he has spoken to us by his Son, whom he appointed heir of all things, and through whom he made the universe" (Heb. 1:2).

Because God knows about and understands dealing with difficult situations and challenging children, he will bless you in your efforts. He will give you strength for each battle. He will grant you his Spirit of patience sufficient for each day. He will not allow you to be tempted beyond what you are able. If all of these sound on some days

> **God knows about difficult situations and challenging children!**

like hollow platitudes, remember what God deals with on a daily basis. This is not so you will try to compare yourself to God; rather, it is so you will understand the source of his empathy and recognize his power to empower you.

You are not alone. Your children and family are not yours alone. Have faith through your special circumstances that God is able to triumph. Keep praying. Keep working. Keep believing. Keep watching. May his blessings pour down upon you and your family like rain.

Father, I trust you to be bigger than my circumstances. I need you to be bigger than my circumstances. When I feel like I can't go on, lead me. When no one around me helps, be my comfort. When I am exhausted, help me lie down and rest. When I have run out of patience, lend me yours. When I think I'm in this battle alone, remind me of your presence. When I have given up on hope, send your Spirit quickly! Amen.

11

Staying on Course

Train a child in the way he should go, and when he is old
he will not turn from it.

Proverbs 22:6

With all my heart, I thank you for working your way through
to this point. Our families today are under attack on so
many different fronts. Your commitment to read through
this book, to implement changes, and to recommit to doing
better for your family's sake are all buffers against the tide
of destruction lapping at the shores of the family unit. As
irresistible as those forces seem, I wanted to start off this
last chapter by reminding you, through the verse above,
of the power of God and the power of promise. God is a
mighty warrior in your corner when it comes to protecting
and guiding your family!

When you picked up this book, your primary concern
may have been an outward one—perhaps you were concerned about what your child ate or how much your child

weighed. *Healthy* kids are so much more than that. Health concerns are certainly appropriate; however, as parents, we must concern ourselves with more than the external, like weight. We must communicate to our children their internal worth in God. And with that thought, we move full circle to the very beginning of this book.

I realize this has been a complex set of issues for you to look at, digest, integrate, and internalize. As a way to help review and provide you with a quick reference for major concepts in the book, I've put together a list for each SOAR concept. As you read them over, you'll be reminded of the important themes presented and have a way to evaluate how you and your family are doing. Each will come in the form of a statement. As you read each statement, personally evaluate the truth in your own life. Commit to living out these statements in the life of your family.

Support

- I motivate my family to change out of love for them.
- I am committed to providing my family with the stability of my love through changes.
- I accept each family member's pace of change, understanding that even a slow pace is progress toward our goals.
- I expect the best from each member of my family every day.
- Understanding my own issues, I make sure to examine my motivations.
- I provide positive verbal support to each member of the family.
- I visualize these changes as permanent.
- I practice daily the support style I identified for myself.

- Through prayer, personal study, meditation, and godly friends, I plug into God's support for me and my family.

Optimism

- I envision a bright future for each member of my family.
- I choose to look to God for hope, not to circumstances.
- I practice patient anticipation and model it to my family.
- I model delayed gratification and show my family the value of waiting.
- I believe in each child's success and accept God's definition of that success.
- I convey to each child, through word and deed, my belief in their future.

Activity

- I foster a positive, can-do attitude with my family.
- I invest my time, energy, and resources in my family's activities.
- I provide each child with plenty of opportunities for daily physical activities.
- I allow the overweight child to grow into his or her weight and do no insist upon losing weight.
- I am a partner with my child's pediatrician regarding physical health.
- I provide a variety of age- and ability-appropriate after-school activities.

- My child is able to receive quality time with me through a significant quantity of time.
- I support my child's schoolwork, both in school and after school.
- I am involved in my child's school through parent groups and/or volunteering.
- Our family has a regular game night or family night when we emphasize our joint family relationship.
- I listen to each child's words and encourage positive self-talk.
- Recognizing the value of a variety of relationships, I encourage and monitor my child's outside acquaintances and friendships.
- Respect for each family member by the family is something I strongly promote by practicing it myself.
- I make a habit of praying with my child.
- I provide an opportunity for my child and I to engage in worship together.
- We read the Bible and talk about God's Word together.
- I incorporate spiritual concepts into my everyday activities and conversations with my child.
- I commit to being an "open book" Christian for my child by practicing spiritual transparency with my family.
- With all of our activities, I recognize the need to allow time for spontaneity.
- I factor in "down time" for my children, especially younger children.
- I purposefully create a restful environment each night to help my children prepare for rest.
- I practice relaxation myself.

Achievement

- I help each child discover his or her God-given talents through exposure to a variety of activities.
- I expect my child to do his or her best, and I emulate this value by doing my best in whatever I do.
- I promote my child's intrinsic motivations as well as acknowledge extrinsic ones.
- My goal for my child is achievement, not perfection.
- I partner with my child's teacher on academic achievement.
- I daily seek opportunities to know my child better.
- I recognize and support my child's learning style.
- I am alert to my child's skills and challenges.
- Through example and Scripture, I teach biblical principles of diligence and hard work.
- I plan to achieve, and I teach my child the same.
- I periodically reevaluate activities for advantages and disadvantages.

Responsibility

- I recognize I am working hard at putting myself out of a job by passing along the characteristics of personal responsibility to my children.
- I provide my children with proper nutrition for each day.
- I model proper nutrition through my own food choices.
- I understand that food is not the answer to every problem in life.
- I recognize that food is not the enemy.

- I live a healthy life myself so I can model it to my children.
- I commit to helping my children eat and drink healthy foods, play hard, and rest well.
- I model moderation and wise decision making when it comes to food choices.
- Regarding my children and certain foods, I think "within limits, not off-limits."
- Each day, I create a clean palate for my child to experience and appreciate good food.
- I provide a variety of healthy snack options.
- I commit to offering three healthy meals each day.
- I encourage the consumption of water.
- While I may occasionally, due to circumstances, operate on "autopilot" nutritionally, I resist the temptation to stay on it too long.
- In a loving way, I communicate the positives and negatives in food choices.
- I think process, not perfection.
- I practice emotional responsibility within my family, in order to model it to my children.
- I am alert to my child's emotional state.
- I allow my child to express emotions.
- I am committed to obtaining professional assistance if my child's healthy emotional state is compromised beyond my ability to help.
- By teaching my child the biblical concepts of salt and light, I promote an attitude of outward service.
- I make it easy for my child to love and respect me.
- I commit to being a monitor and a mirror for my child.
- Like any good commander, I choose my battles carefully.

- I regularly evaluate my relationship with my child and seek always to improve myself.
- I model my faith.
- I extend, seek, and accept forgiveness.
- By going to church, I give my family the gift of a spiritual community.
- I commit to providing healthy spiritual soil within my family for our faith to grow and flourish.

A God-Designed Whole Person

Each child is a whole person, created by God to be an emotional, relational, physical, and spiritual being. When these aspects are addressed, your child truly can SOAR! You can do this—in small and large ways, day by day, you can do this! You needn't do it perfectly, but you should do it consistently. As your family makes baby steps, walk right with them. Take those steps yourself and recognize you're in it together.

> You needn't be perfect, but you should be **consistent**.

Above all, continue to communicate your love and support—through your words, your actions, your commitment. Lead your family where you want them to go. Embody the qualities you want them to exhibit. You truly have more power for good than you imagine.

Remember the true source of that power for good: "Now to him who is able to do immeasurably more than all we ask or imagine, according to his power that is at work within us, to him be glory in the church and in Christ Jesus throughout all generations, for ever and ever! Amen" (Eph. 3:20–21). Yes, God's power is immeasurable; he is able to do more than all we ask or imagine. So start imagining a healthier life for your family! Keep asking him for guidance and help. Allow his power to be at work within you as you work with your family. Give all glory to Jesus for the positive changes in your life.

Dear Father, I give you praise for your power to change lives for the better. Be with me each day as this family I love becomes even healthier than it is today. I thank you for your vision of hope, and I acknowledge all the good you have done. When I falter, sustain me. When I stumble, pick me up. When I achieve, accept my praise. In failure and in victory, help me to stay the course and allow my family to SOAR! Amen.

Resource List

Instruct a wise man and he will be wiser still.

Proverbs 9:9

The following additional resources are presented to you as a way to augment what you've learned in SOAR. Each one has a unique perspective and may be of use to you and your family. They are listed alphabetically by the author's last name, with a short review paragraph. You'll notice that most of the books approach this subject from a "weight" perspective, and most are not written from a Christian perspective. However, each has strengths that can be harvested and incorporated into your family patterns.

In addition to the resources reviewed below, you might also benefit from reading two of my books, which have offered help and hope to readers for almost ten years. The first is *Hope, Help, and Healing for Eating Disorders*. This book is extremely helpful if you recognize that someone in your family (including yourself) has an issue with food, weight, and body image. It is written from a biblical perspective and presents the topic of eating disorders, from anorexia to bulimia to binge eating to compulsive overeating, in a whole person way.

The second book is *Healing the Scars of Emotional Abuse*. This book would be very helpful if you recognize that you are perpetuating in your own family any destructive family patterns. Your family cannot SOAR if they are tied down by negativism, criticism, pessimism, and the shackles of emotional abuse. If you have been damaged by emotional abuse in your own past, I encourage you to get this book and experience healing so you'll be better able to minister to your own family.

Your top resource, of course, will always be the Bible, which is a conduit for the wisdom and guidance of God. Find a translation you like that speaks to you personally. Prayerfully consider the other resources listed here. And may God bless your continued efforts to bring up healthy and happy children.

Berg, Frances M. *Underage and Overweight: America's Childhood Obesity Crisis—What Every Family Needs to Know*. Long Island City, NY: Hatherleigh Press, 2004. If you're feeling like your child's size is all your fault—you need to read this book. It outlines the multiple reasons for childhood obesity and offers practical and realistic solutions. One of the best chapters is entitled "Seven Steps to a Healthier Weight," which incorporates many of the whole-person principles found in SOAR. This is not a Christian book, so it must be filtered through biblical insights and understanding.

Cederquist, Caroline J. *Helping Your Overweight Child: A Family Guide*. Naples, FL: Advance Medical Press, 2002. Through the example of "K.C." and her family, Dr. Cederquist outlines societal influences on obesity and the role of the entire family in adopting healthy habits. Her presentation is straightforward and easy to read. The appendices, which take up almost the second half of the book, include information on helpful journaling of habits, the different options available at popular fast-food restaurants, a listing of "kid favorite" foods such as pizza and all kinds of cereals with nutrition facts, definitions of words used on food labels, and a recipe section from her own kitchen. This book also has an alphabetized index for easy cross-referencing.

Cooper, Kenneth H. *Fit Kids! The Complete Shape-Up Program from Birth through High School.* Nashville: Broadman & Holman Publishers, 1991, 1999. Dr. Cooper is the founder of the Cooper Institute, a nonprofit educational and research facility based in Dallas, Texas. One of the institute's main focuses is on the relationship between living habits and overall health. If you're looking for a resource to help you create a detailed exercise and eating plan for your child, from birth to teenager, this book is full of ideas, charts, and medical information. An extensive reference list can help you find journal and periodical information. Topics are indexed alphabetically.

Dalton, Sharron. *Our Overweight Children: What Parents, Schools, and Communities Can Do to Control the Fatness Epidemic.* Berkeley, CA: University of California Press, 2004. This is a handbook of sorts on advocacy for children in our communities and schools. It outlines the sources and complicating factors in childhood obesity and suggests different approaches for children with regard to food and physical activities. This book would be helpful for any parent wanting to engage in "battle" with schools, day care facilities, or the community at large over issues relating to childhood obesity.

Friedman, Sandra Susan. *When Girls Feel Fat: Helping Girls Through Adolescence.* Buffalo, NY: Firefly Books, 2000. While many other books deal primarily with weight issues from a diet and exercise point of view, this book deals with the *perception* of fat. The pressure to be thin and the perception of being fat are culturally irresistible. In a world where eating disorders are rising for both girls and boys, this book is especially important if you have a preadolescent or adolescent girl. In my counseling agency, this book is a standard resource for assisting parents to help navigate their daughters through this awkward time of life.

Gavin, Mary L., Steven A. Dowshen, and Neil Izenberg. *FitKids: A Practical Guide to Raising Healthy and Active Children—from Birth to Teens.* New York: DK Publishing, Inc, 2004. This book was prepared by the medical staff at KidsHealth.org, a children's health website. It's a colorful book full of bright pictures and organized into age categories from birth to teenagers. It has special sections on children with food allergies and the needs of the child athlete. Although it gives mainly an overview type of presentation, it also offers helpful tips and recipes. It's the type of book you can keep on hand to review age-specific information as your child grows.

Levine, Judith, and Linda Bine. *Helping Your Child Lose Weight the Healthy Way: A Family Approach to Weight Control.* Sacramento: Citadel Press, 1996, 2001. This book is by a registered dietician and consultant for the American Heart Association. As such, its emphases are diet and exercise for your child, though it does touch on self-esteem issues. It includes helpful advice on how to start an exercise program for your child as well as a number of easy-to-prepare recipes developed with the preferences of children in mind. The biggest plus for this book is the way it presents a child's weight within a family context, marshalling family resources to deal with this issue.

Rimm, Dr. Sylvia, with Dr. Eric Rimm. *Rescuing the Emotional Lives of Overweight Children: What Our Kids Go Through—And How We Can Help.* New York: Rodale, 2004. While this book is written specifically to address the emotional impact on children of being overweight, it provides stories and insights valuable for everyone. If you were overweight as a child yourself and are now reliving that anguish through your own child, this book will help you help your child. Though written from a secular perspective, alert Christians will be able to see God's wisdom displayed through the commonsense solutions.

Sears, William, and Peter Sears, with Sean Foy. *Dr. Sears' LEAN Kids.* New York: New American Library, 2003. Written by father-and-son physicians, this book uses the acronym LEAN to emphasize Lifestyle, Exercise, Attitude, and Nutrition. This book does a good job of addressing each area in an easy-to-follow format. It emphasizes the role of parents as "wellness coaches." This book does not address a spiritual aspect but does offer some helpful exercises and dietary tips.

Southern, Melinda S., T. Kristian von Almen, and Heidi Schumacher. *Trim Kids.* New York: Harper Resource, 2001.

This book basically outlines a trademarked weight management program for children. Each week a different strategy is introduced and integrated into the program. If you're looking for a structured, paced presentation, this may be a helpful book. This book gives a limited presentation of emotional and relational factors, but it does give helpful suggestions for diet and exercise.

Thompson, Colleen, and Ellen Shanley. *Overcoming Childhood Obesity*. Boulder, CO: Bull Publishing Co., 2004. This book is full of helpful, specific advice, from the top ten healthy behaviors for teenagers to modified food pyramids for ethnic eating to a detailed discussion of macronutrients, vitamins, and minerals. It has an alphabetized index in the back, and the pages have bold, large print with lots of space around the margins for notes. A section on children in the kitchen outlines age-appropriate activities, and the book gives a variety of recipes for healthy eating.

2 to 20 years: Boys
Body mass index-for-age percentiles

NAME _____

RECORD # _____

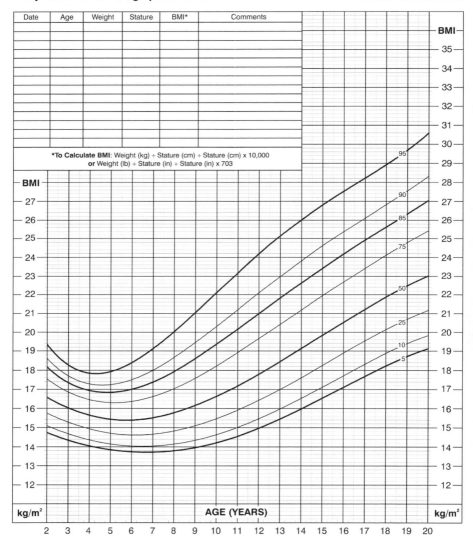

Date	Age	Weight	Stature	BMI*	Comments

*To Calculate BMI: Weight (kg) ÷ Stature (cm) ÷ Stature (cm) x 10,000
or Weight (lb) ÷ Stature (in) ÷ Stature (in) x 703

AGE (YEARS)

Published May 30, 2000 (modified 10/16/00).

SOURCE: Developed by the National Center for Health Statistics in collaboration with
the National Center for Chronic Disease Prevention and Health Promotion (2000).
http://www.cdc.gov/growthcharts

SAFER · HEALTHIER · PEOPLE™

2 to 20 years: Girls
Body mass index-for-age percentiles

NAME _____

RECORD # _____

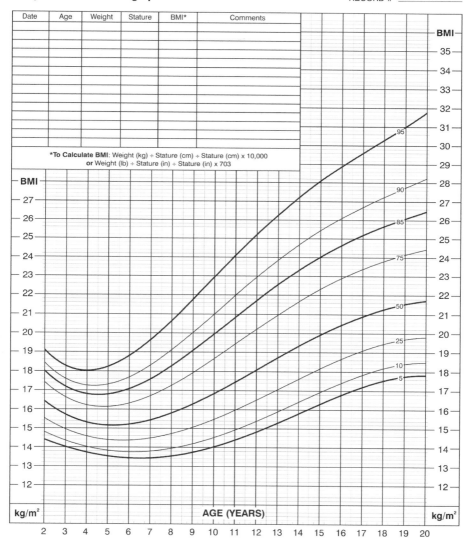

Date	Age	Weight	Stature	BMI*	Comments

*To Calculate BMI: Weight (kg) ÷ Stature (cm) ÷ Stature (cm) x 10,000
or Weight (lb) ÷ Stature (in) ÷ Stature (in) x 703

BMI

AGE (YEARS)

kg/m²

Published May 30, 2000 (modified 10/16/00).
SOURCE: Developed by the National Center for Health Statistics in collaboration with
the National Center for Chronic Disease Prevention and Health Promotion (2000).
http://www.cdc.gov/growthcharts

SAFER · HEALTHIER · PEOPLE

Too much math to figure out your child's BMI? Go to www.kidshealth.org/parent/growth/growth/bmi_charts.html and scroll down the page to "The KidsHealth BMI Calculator." Put in gender, date of birth, and date of measurement, with height and weight. It will give you your child's BMI. After the child's BMI has been calculated, use the graph to plot his or her age and BMI. The "wavy" lines are average percentiles for age. For example, Amy is an eight-year-old girl with a BMI of 18. She is in the 80+ percentile for weight, meaning more than 80 percent of children her age weigh less and less than 20 percent weigh more. Percentiles are used by pediatricians, and your child's pediatrician can help you determine the optimum percentile range for your child.

Gregory L. Jantz, Ph.D., is a popular speaker and an award-winning author. He is a certified chemical dependency professional, a nationally certified psychologist, and a nationally certified eating disorder specialist. Dr. Jantz is the founder and executive director of The Center for Counseling and Health Resources, Inc., a leading mental health and chemical dependency treatment facility with five clinics in the Seattle, Washington, area.

The Center for Counseling and Health Resources, Inc., is a full-service counseling center and also acts as a referral and information source for those seeking help for a variety of mental health issues. The Center specializes in whole-person care, with individuals from across the United States and around the world coming to participate in the hope-filled work of recovery. Dr. Jantz's whole-person approach addresses the emotional, relational, intellectual, physical, and spiritual dimensions of each person with a unique, tailored treatment plan. Over the past twenty years, Dr. Jantz and The Center have treated nearly seven thousand people with all types of disorders using the successful whole-person approach.

Dr. Jantz's compassionate, solution-oriented viewpoints on timely topics, plus his natural gift for storytelling, make him a sought-after guest on local and national radio and television. He speaks nationally at conferences, seminars, and retreats on a wide variety of topics, utilizing his extensive expertise and experience. Dr. Jantz has also hosted several popular live call-in radio shows, participating in well over a thousand individual interviews since 1995.

Dr. Jantz has authored numerous best-selling books, including a book used in the treatment of eating disorders, *Hope, Help, and Healing for Eating Disorders*. His other books include *Losing Weight Permanently: Secrets of the 2% Who Succeed; The Spiritual Path to Weight Loss; 21 Days to Eating Better; Becoming Strong Again; Hidden Dangers of the Internet; Too Close to the Flame: Recognizing and Avoiding Sexualized Relationships;* and *Turning the Tables on Gambling: Hope and Help for an Addictive Behavior.*

Dr. Jantz hosts a monthly audiotape club on the topic of eating disorders called the Hope Series. This resource is sent monthly to subscribers from across the United States and provides cutting-edge nutritional information, new advances in the treatment of eating disorders, inspiration to aid healing, and practical suggestions for ongoing recovery.

Dr. Jantz has been married for twenty years to his wife, LaFon. They have been blessed with two sons, Gregg and Benjamin.

Ann McMurray is a freelance writer living in Mountlake Terrace, Washington. She has worked with Dr. Jantz on *Healing the Scars of Emotional Abuse; Hope, Help, and Healing for Eating Disorders; Hidden Dangers of the Internet; Too Close to the Flame: Recognizing and Avoiding Sexualized Relationships; Turning the Tables on Gambling: Hope and Help for an Addictive Behavior;* and *Moving Beyond Depression.*

McMurray's partnership with Dr. Jantz also extends to The Center for Counseling and Health Resources, Inc., where she works as operations assistant.

She has been married to her husband, Tad, for twenty-seven years and has two children, Joel and Lindsay.

For more information about resources related to developing a healthy lifestyle, or to speak to someone, you may call The Center's toll-free number, (888) 771-5166. For more information about The Center or to receive information about speaking engagements with Dr. Jantz, go to www.aplaceofhope.com or write to The Center for Counseling and Health Resources, Inc., P.O. Box 700, Edmonds, WA 98020.

Find Freedom from Yo-Yo Dieting

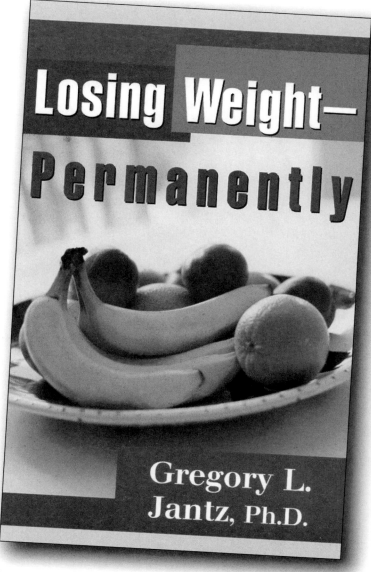

Losing Weight— Permanently

Gregory L. Jantz, Ph.D.

ℛ Revell
www.revellbooks.com